CULTURE TRUMPS STRATEGY
BREAK THE MYTH

TRANSFORMING BUSINESS? TRANSFORM THE MIND FIRST

MADHUSUDAN DUTTA

INDIA • SINGAPORE • MALAYSIA

ISBN 979-8-89133-753-4

Om Sai Baba

22.4.21.

The stories about leadership dynamics mentioned in this book are based on real events, but the names of the companies and characters are concealed/masked.

CONTENTS

ACKNOWLEDGEMENTS

This book is a symbiotic effort of many minds. While it was just penned down through me, it's not mine alone. Capturing the diverse elements of unique ideas from the organizations I was associated with as well as the various leadership guru's I had the opportunity to interact with, has been an extremely exciting journey.

I have always penned my thoughts into a journal that I carry around, which has been my go to mantra since the beginning of my professional journey in leadership role. It was only during the pandemic that I pulled out some of these older memoirs (rather rustic covered in dust) and thought, why not translate these scattered experiences into one concise book. It is important to mention that these ideas and experiences, which have translated into this book is that's to the encouragement from my esteemed guru's, colleagues, mentors, friends without whom this book would not have seen the light of day.

With humility, I acknowledge the insight I gained from my mentors of the Industry, who had kindly devoted time to sharpen my saw in gaining knowledge. I'm eternally grateful specifically to two stalwarts of the academic world – Dr Radhakrishnan Pillai, the eminent author on Chanakya's wisdom based leadership. Dr Pillai's pep talk at a relevant moment unfolded a new horizon of opportunities for first time authors like me. Grateful to you Doc.

I would also like to acknowledge the contribution of Dr Nigel Nicholson, the eminent educator, thinker, author and also the ex- professor of organization behaviour at the London Business School (LBS). He played a vital role in pushing me beyond my expectations (in life).

My appreciation is also to the abundance of knowledge of Dr Rashmi Sharma, the behavioural science specialist from London Business School. Rakesh Bhutoria, an alumni of London school of economics & political science, alumni of also SP Jain institute, one of the classy MD/ CEO I came across,.

I am fortunate to have the encouragement of my family members' - Mala(wife), Medha, Maurya, and friends' Somesh, Sanjib, Dhruv they were instrumental in lifting me every time I experienced 'writer's block'.

I am grateful beyond words, to have received endless support from my whole team, my esteemed colleagues, close friends and relatives. Those refreshing sessions over a steaming cup of "First Flush Darjeeling" tea showed me the way forward.

And of course, let me kneel down before my late parents, late parents in- law who will never be able to read this book but must be smiling from the heaven as finally I could produce this book.

Last but not the least, I must express my gratitude to you – the reader, for picking up this book and giving it a chance. I am hopeful that you will find it interesting and possibly find some parallel to my life journey.

1

NAVIGATING BUSINESS AMIDST A TURBULENT SEA – CAN YOUR FUNDAMENTAL VALUES BE YOUR LIGHTHOUSE?

Learning story from the Global giant MNC

The Chowringhee! The heart of the city of joy - a signature of the city - rather, the heartbeat of Kolkata.

Strolling leisurely in the sunny afternoon at the onset of spring, around March '90, I got soaked in enjoying the iconic old - colonial era buildings of this former British capital. What an elegance of the extra ordinary, elaborated architecture of few of the iconic buildings of the British regime. The city's 'grande dames' in this Chowringhee area still hold considerable sway in its cultural life.

Cacophony of all sort of noise, plenty of hawkers hollering with their products by occupying almost the entire walkway amidst flow of huge movements of all sort of people. The honking of the iconic yellow cab, noise from the umpteen number of buses, vehicles leading to the unceasing stream of traffic on the Chowringhee road, long signals, madding crowd, bit of pollution in the air created an intriguing scenario. At times it's literally tough to walk through. But no worries, no complaints as it describes the spirit of the city of joy.

Amazingly, few from the crowds appeared to have mastered the art of ignoring the traffic signal and dared in crossing over the busiest road amidst intense traffic movements like Moses parting the Red Sea!

They won't have the patience to wait for the red light of the traffic signal while crossing over the busiest street! Would you term them impatient folks? Chivalry? Would you perceive them as skilled folks in intercepting the high traffic movements while crossing over the street with high risk? Was it an attitude of breaking the norms? But that's the way they are.

Visualising what possibly could be the gorgeous canvas of the opposite side of Chowringhee from the top floors of the towering buildings on the main road, I crossed over to the opposite side - the maidan area (vast lash green Brigade Parade ground) . Its contrast - a different world altogether. The bright blue sky of spring is fascinating. The lash green Maidan area - full of giant trees, bushes and smaller plants with flowers. Strolling around the green grass, my conscious mind travelled from row upon rows of huge trees. It went to the furthest point of the vast maidan. The trees seems to be vibrantly alive. The trees at the furthest point seems to be standing very close to each other communicating and hugging each other. Soothing breeze of the maidan area coupled with its silence had a calming effect in the ambience. Being spring, the tiny green leaves started to sprout from the buds. Happiness was pouring within me. I remembered the lovely quote of **Angela Abraham (*****)**:

"There is hope in the spring day, hope in the new green growth that flourishes upon the earth. I feel the warmth in the breeze that was not there few days ago. I sense the days are becoming lighter and brighter. And there is the bud upon the optimistic branch, brave enough to bring forth such delicate leaves and open them in to the sunshine".

It's greenness would refresh any fatigued soul. I came closer to one of the most popular super star hotel of the Chowringhee, the most gracious building reflecting the Victorian architecture. The glamourous top brand hotel stood out to be classy amidst those series of buildings.

But a sudden jerk in my mind took me to a trip down the memory lane of an episode in this same super star hotel some three decades back! Oh it was dreadful - one can't forget that horrible afternoon. Incidentally, that was a spring noon too!

Learning episode 1

From one of the best - in - class MNC – a global pharmaceutical and health care giant!!

The usual quarterly business review of the leading giant multinational pharmaceutical company was being conducted on the first floor banquet hall of this super star hotel. The marketing and product team leaders from the head quarter and the local leading sales executives were present. The agenda was packed. The ambiance was that of a typical business review that the leading MNCs use to follow and the format was simple - the review of the last quarter's business performance and strategy to achieve the next quarter's business target. The schedule was moving like a well - orchestrated show. It was around twelve noon. Amidst such progress, two junior executives who just entered the venue rushing towards the head table and whispered with tensed faces to the three leaders conducting the programme about the huge gathering of the executive's trade union and their possible agitation against us! They also could figure out that there was hardly any of our company's representatives in the melee. The mob gathered was apparently from a leading external union having members mostly from other organisations. In fact, one of the agenda for this association for a long time had been to seek recognition from the company. The company as a matter of principle believed in recognising internal union only. The internal union had a soft corner for this external forum but nothing official about it!!

Well, in the meantime, the security in- charge of the hotel too rushed towards our conference hall. In a flash of moments the news spread that around three hundred members of one of the leading executive union of the eastern region rather the entire country had already thronged inside the hotel overruling the resistance of the security personnel. Shouting of slogans could be clearly heard of from the Banquet. The demand was that the three key leaders conducting the show must come down to meet the agitators and the company must withdraw the termination notice served to one of the company's sales executive.

Panic mounted up. The guests were tensed. Few of the guests appeared to be from overseas were rushing for safe shelters. The bewildered hotel staff appeared to be seen running. The loud noise from shouting of slogans scaled up. More security guards assembled near the reception with the object to prevent the demonstrators climbing up the stairs. The company's business leaders pressed the hotel authority to call for police intervention specially when the executives union were well known for their taking tough stand, and had a strong affiliation with a leading political banner of the country.

The high strung episode of the next few minutes were unbelievably strange! The strong three hundred plus agitators simply overpowered the resistance from the security personnel and the agitated mob shouting vociferous slogans barged in to the meeting venue. In twinkle of seconds the mob almost ransacked the venue. Our three bewildered and highly tensed executives had no option but made efforts to flee from the venue. But the front runners of the agitators got hold of them. We experienced the futile but brave efforts of company's few other colleagues to ring fence the three leaders. The mob almost became violent demanding from their union leaders leading the agitation, all sort of possible actions against those company executives. In a quickest possible time consensus appeared amongst them that three company senior executives be dragged by the agitators towards the other hotel where another business division's quarterly review was going on. The venue was just within one and half kilometres away and that was a renowned hotel brand too. The tensed but curious onlookers with their strange sense could witness the strong agitators forced and dragged the company's three senior executives to follow them through a procession walking through the busiest Chowringhee - the heart of the city. The public in general, the curious passengers from buses and vehicles kept pondering while the highly tensed, helpless three executives with formal business dresses had no option but to walk along with the agitators amidst constant slogans! Amidst shouting of slogans, few of the hyperactive agitators kept on frequently screaming at the three executives with filthy languages. All of a sudden, two of the younger guys rushed towards a pan (betel) stall-picked up the scissor while others slowed down the pace little bit. Two hyperactive guys moved very close to the executives. One of them to the utter surprise of everyone, got hold of the neck tie of the executives and the other folk used the scissor and cut the tie it to two pieces. Protest by the company executives were booed down and same frightening action were applied to all three senior executives. The height of humiliation.

In the meantime, the rest of the company executives left the venue to move back to zonal office possibly to communicate with higher authorities at the head office. They apparently informed the police authorities too seeking intervention including informing them about the possible venue that the agitators were marching towards. They also informed the police about how the company executives were constantly heckled and humiliated in the streets amidst broad day light.

In about fifteen minutes, the agitators reached their destination to the other venue. The number of agitators by that time swelled up which clearly reflected the strong bonding of the unionists.

- Was it camaraderie?
- Was it an effort in safe guarding the socio - economic justice of one of their comrade?
- Was it high commitment to establish the union's objectives and agenda?
- Was it an aggressive negotiation technique to cow down the strong opponent?
- Was it is big bully to press home their demand?
- Was it a ploy to show case union's strength to influence management's agreeing to such union's recognition?
- Was it that individual's behaviour got impacted by the influence of mob psychology
- Was it that individuals lost their self-identity and were heavily influenced by the loss of responsibility of the individual as the increasing crowd size and their increasing agitation also created impact?

Police authorities having secured the information in advance could be seen at the next spot where the agitators reached. The ambience around the main gate was getting highly tensed. To our utter surprise the agitators forced their entry to the reception and lounge area and subsequently to the banquet room where the other business division's important quarterly business review was being conducted. The agitators disrupting the proceedings, forced the meeting to be suspended-compelled the rest of the executives to leave the spot at once and got hold of few senior leaders conducting the review. Demand was clear and that was the withdrawal of the termination order of the sales executive. The police officers could persuade the agitators through discussions that the company executives be allowed to leave but not before the leaders of the union obtaining an assurance that local management would inform the top management about their demand and invite the union representatives for joint discussions.

The highly depressed, dejected, discontented senior leaders after taking care of few formalities of lodging compliant etc decided to get back to office together. Being though in a state of ramshackle, what charmed me was the spirit in them as they never could accept such brutality and I could hear the echo of their mind - confronting such offensive acts!

From nowhere my mind like a flash could recall an interesting citation from eminent print and media professional, **'Vir Sanghvi' (****)** that "**Calcutta is not for everyone. You want your cities clean and green, stick to Delhi. You want your cities, rich and impersonal, go to Bombay. You want them to be high- tech and full of draught beer; Bangalore's your place. But if you want a city with a soul, come to Calcutta".** Would information of such an episode could have impacted Vir Sanghvi to alter his views? Well, let's not generalise the situations. But the way company executives braved the toughest situations had provoked us to ponder on:

Would we term such mind set of company executives who faced the humiliation but didn't break, as an attitude of resilience?

would we view such attributes as right traits of leadership and demonstrate that true leaders can't buckle under pressure?

While trade unions have every right to air their grievances, stage strong protests, demand withdrawal of biased action of management but would not such acts be construed as unacceptable under the alibi of unionism?

With a fatigued mind and body, I was returning home through the 'Red road' - the famous spacious road known for its charming greeneries on both side of the road. Arrival of spring could be felt from the surroundings - a season that is known to make people happy. Spring brings more day light and I could recall an expert's opinion that increased day light also sparks the release of serotonin, a chemical from our brain which fosters happiness. Happiness? Goodness of spring? Alas – The presence of spring around the greeneries no way could charm as the unruly agitation created a scar in my mind.

Earnest Hemingway (*****) rightly expressed:

"When spring came, even the false spring, there were no problems except where to be happiest. The only thing that could spoil a day was people,

and if you could keep from making engagements, each day had no limits.

People were always the limiters of happiness except for the very few that were as good as spring itself."

Focus point:

Neuroscientist's discovery that when we suddenly recall past interesting memories, a representation of the entire event is instantaneously reactivated in the brain. Interestingly, brain facilitates us to even recall the location, people, or any other small memorabilia! Once we get in to such syndrome of recalling such old memories, the episodes through flash back like a film could portray vivid recollections. Yes – interesting indeed.

And therefore, I could easily correlate why those scintillating episodes even after two and half decades flashed clearly to my memory.

Most interesting was the opportunity to get the views, analysis of how our corporate leadership viewed such type of agitation which became an interesting subject in the corporate corridors chat. And we could listen from none other than two corporate stalwarts about the above episode - Anal Matekar and Praveen Nayek. This was when we met them in a workshop at Lonawala may be just an year after the episode.

My memory could recall one of the great evening we had on the final day's workshop in that lounge of the resort. On our request, both the corporate seniors had agreed to exchange views on that controversial episodes as most of us were keen to learn all possible strategic angles. And it was this two senior leaders from HQ who had effectively dealt with that most sensitive issues we had witnessed in Zonal HQ.

So, I raised the first point of curiosity with Anal and here goes the crux of the key conversations:

MSD – So Anal.....Being zonal Head Quarter (ZHQ) guys, we use to be mentored and guided by the Corporate leadership team. You and Praveen beside being boss also played mentors role too while grooming the ZHQ Human Resources team. We at ZHQ were partially shattered, confused, tensed with the fall out of that sudden high - voltage actions. We were uncertain as to where are we heading to?

But Corporate Head Quarters (CHQ) swung in to action without wasting a single moment. And we all knew that the strategy to deal with the sensitive issues were mainly navigated by you two. The CHQ leadership team's decision to rush to ZHQ on the very next day where beside both of you, our Director Human Resources and Director Marketing's also flew down. That itself brought us huge comfort and feelings that how serious you were to deal with the possible consequences arising out of the unprecedented agitation which drew the attention of the print media too.

So, I am keen to understand what was some of the strategy that you all together worked out in the emergency meetings you had before taking flights to Kolkata? The challenge was galore since it involved 'revenue versus discipline' – Therefore, won't it be interesting to gain from the learning perspectives?

A quick sip of the single malt by Anal! Creative lighting at the lounge, soft music, personal touch of the bar attendant while serving us, had already created an interesting ambience which made all of us comfortable.

Praveen's grinning had an inner significance while he apparently was trying to get soaked in to the spirit of single malt while blending his thoughts on the topics. Both appeared to be glancing in to their flash back mode. A pause - silence prevailed for few seconds and then Anal got in to conversation mode!

AM – Well, it's difficult indeed to recall strategies we adopted as incident happened long back. But yes, the episode had an unexpected scar on many. Yea – let me try to recall and share the finer aspects. A pause ....and Anal continued.

The key strategies were clear -

- Communication meeting with the key leaders at corporate including getting engaged with internal Union leaders too.
- Keeping the Board Members in the loop.
- Focus on keeping communication channel transparent, open, both with employees and external stakeholders since the issue was quite serious in nature as you rightly said that it involved 'both revenues and discipline and how one deals with Core Values.
- Corporate communication and PR team was all along with us during key discussions and played key role ensuring effective communication was maintained.

Well, let Praveen contribute now and let me do justice to the single malt and simultaneously try and glance down my memory lane to recall few more key points.

PN – Thanks MSD for provoking us! We already are making effort to ignite and tease our brains in recalling the points you wanted us to share. I guess what influenced us at that point of time was collectively we brought on the table the key issues and debated rather questioned ourselves collectively. Idea was perhaps to see that we all were on the same page while seeking answers to the issues we talked about. Answers we got, made it easy for all of us to navigate the complexity. The points we deliberated were:

☞ Which sector of Industry we were operating?

A - Purely pharmaceuticals and health care products.

☞ Who were our customers or rather consumers?

A - The patients.

☞ What were our products?

A - Purely important medicines, health care products including life - saving drugs.

☞ Who would patronize our products?

A - It was the medical fraternity – the Doctors, including the leading specialists dealing with health and life of the patients.

☞ What influences the patients - more importantly the entire Doctor's community to rely on our products?

A – Simple: The Brand image. The trust and reliability on our products across the country rather across entire universe wherever we are present. Importantly, also our strong global presence including quality consciousness, supremacy in R & D were huge factors in gaining the trust of the consumers. Therefore, people's including consumers had complete trust on our Core Values that the company has created over decades.

The collective views of the leadership team was unanimous on one of the point the trust which the consumers and the ailing patients had on their brand and products had was above everything. Well, once such fundamental issues were addressed clearly, we all felt the power of "empowerment from within". One can then comfortably deal with any complex issues.

"Your Core Values need to be the lighthouse in the event business is confronted with highly complex situations".

"If you are not willing to accept the pain real values incur, don't bother going to the trouble of formulating a values statement". (from HBR review).

Though it was an episode of quite some time back, but we remember pretty clearly the courses we followed. There would have been many other important actions and strategies, but let me highlight the fundamentals.

AM – Praveen made the tasks easier. He highlighted the broad concept. He has elaborated on the foundational principles and let me touch upon the fundamental principles that we adopted while meeting various forums at Kolkata:

- Foremost was effective communications with local government machineries expressing our keenness to continue to contribute to the healthcare sectors in that part of the country.
- This was necessary in view of the medical fraternities specially the Doctors including the specialists, consumers – ailing patients, huge distribution network related people, retailers involvement and trust on our brand. Therefore, we wanted to express our commitment to continue to support one of the most important sector – the health care.
- But we wanted to share our devotion in ensuring ethical standard including our commitment to ethical behaviour which were key to our building brand image over a period of time and that too

in the business of manufacturing and distribution of medicines including life – saving drugs.

- Therefore, we wanted to emphasise that termination order should stand since it had followed the laid down principles of natural justice.
- The misconduct committed by the sales executives were not only serious but contravened the spirit and essence of the company's Core Values.
- Appropriate communication were shared conveying integrity reflects that all employees act with honesty and with right conduct. It's critical and hence decisions are not reversible.
- The company beside vehemently condemning the rowdy behaviours against its executives during the unprecedented agitation would seek justice from appropriate authorities including initiating legal and criminal steps.
- We also sought assurance of safety and security to company's executives and its properties.
- Consciousness was very high and clear. Let's remember - Industry is watching you. Market is watching you. Doctors community, customers, consumers, patients are watching you. Your distributors of products, your retailers dealing with your products are watching you, Your investors are also keenly watching you. Your vendor partners are watching you. Your competitors are watching you. Governance machineries are watching you –

What else could have been more important than taking adequate care of your business philosophies and frame work of principles in which you would like to operate under such situations?

The DNA of any organization is tested especially when you are amidst complex situations. So was in our case too.

Therefore, the decision making process of the leadership team was clear. Compromising with any guiding principles could help in gaining from a short term perspective. But ultimately from the mid or long term perspectives, it's wise to stick to your principles which includes sticking to your Core Values.

☞ Such philosophy across the company's global establishments is well established. That's key to the company image, the Brand value, the morale and motivation of the internal and external stakeholders which in turn would facilitate attaining newer heights.

While thanking both the stalwarts profusely for their wonderful articulations on strategic issues of one of the most talked about episode of the Industry during those time, I could recall the interesting quote of **Jensen Huang (****)** which seems to be apt over here as he said –

"I don't think you can create culture and develop Core Values during great times. I think it's when the company faces adversity of extraordinary proportions, when there's no reason for the company to survive, when you are looking at incredible odds – that's when culture is developed, character is developed."

What an interesting evening session it was!

Withholding the values –

Successful organisation's foundations are on established Core Values. Core values are perceived by the employees as the guiding principles in driving business and behaviours. The confluence of core values helps in building corporate culture, work ethics. Beside facilitating in building those key points, the core values provides the foundation for a sound business. With its strong presence, the business would flourish even in difficult times but without its presence the business might see short term result but can't flourish in the mid and long term. Well, organisations usually involves its members while developing the Core Values but usually five to six are the numbers that gets accepted as Core Values.

The challenge is not to select or identify the core values or communicating the same to employees. The challenge is how you integrate or align every members to each of the defined Core Values. How you ensure that every members are soaked and bleached in the spirit of defined Values. Once that is achieved, organisations would create its foot prints amongst the most admired companies. Each stake holder would feel pride in withholding the spirit of the Core Values. Customers would appreciate the importance to be associated with such organization. The brand value would be perceived like "owners pride - neighbours envy"!

Ratan N Tata wonderfully crafted his views on importance of core values when he said - "Business, as I have seen it, places one great demand on you; it needs you to self- impose a frame work of ethics, values, fairness and objectivity on yourself at all times".

Once the Core Values are established, it will help in distinguishing the company's identity and what it cares for. It would massively help in:

a. shaping company's culture

b. attract right talents as professionals would always prefer the company to stand for its core values

c. retentions of employees becomes easier

d. helps the authorities in decision making processes

e. strong presence of core values educate or bring awareness to clients and potential customers about what the company stands for and in today's complex market, it's a competitive advantage

f. overall success on a long term perspective

It's all about the effective leadership to navigate the organization when there are dilemma or complex business situations.

In this organization, we have learnt that the leaders across business, owned up the responsibility of facilitating their team members to internalise the values of the Core Values. And another interesting view came forward was:

Well – Would it be true to say that established MNCs with their strong presence globally having strong revenue base could express such firmness rather uncompromising attitude in dealing with such situations?

Or was it a MNC culture where such consciousness on organisational values stemmed or got developed over decades from their Global Head – Quarters?

Or was it the influence of 'values first versus revenues subsequently' since you are dealing with products linked to people's health?

And gradually over a period of time, such principles got embodied in the DNA of the organisation and you create your identity in the market place?

Key take home - Ethical leadership precedes business sustainability.

Learning episode 2

☞ **From the leading FMCG – An Indian Multinational encompassing episode on Revenues - Core Values – hostilities.**

An early morning call from my Director Human Resource on a 'Asthami' day of the auspicious Durga Puja waked me up in our Delhi residence during my four days of planned leave. 'Bongs' across the country swings in to the festive mood during this four days. My boss cajoling call influenced me to proceed to our elegant office - our head quarter, bit early for an urgent meeting with the top three leaders including our CEO - the glamorous leader of the FMCG world - an IIT, IIM alumni. The century plus company was the leading FMCG brand and the uncrowned king in that sector.

My mind was already apprehensive of possible agenda that was about to be unfolded as I was aware of the brewing up of disputes between our sales forces and the state union of the strong field executives association in the state of Kerala. So, the meeting started much before the office time.

"look my friend - we are extremely sorry to have bothered you specifically during your leave due to Durga Puja. But we felt you are our ' man Friday ' on resolving issues that we are having in

Kerala. Being Ayurvedic centric state in health care product area, our revenues are significantly high in Kerala but you are aware that how badly the revenue is dipping due to our tussle with that state sales representative's union. They are hardly allowing our field force to work in the market. In the last two days they gheraoed our sales manager and branch manager in the market place for more than two hours when finally the local police intervened and gherao was lifted which you are aware of. And yesterday morning they have submitted their demands and action plan which includes threatening to launch state wise agitation in support of their demands to withdraw show cause notices of few of our erring field executives for their performance issues. They are planning to disrupt supply chain activities by agitating at the state wise whole seller's and distributor's points. Before it becomes more complex, we need you to rush there to resolve the issues. Yes - it's a discipline related issue but we can't afford to see our competitors grab the opportunity and push their products".

The articulative CEO knew how to ignite his leaders while assigning challenging assignments. But never forgot to share his emotions as being a 'bong' I was surely going to miss the festivity - the most important one for the 'gourmand bongs' as these four days beside the puja, their passion of displaying gastronomist skill steals the show.

Demoralising the festive spirit of the family members, I moved on! The three hours flying time to Kochi engaged me in an internal monologue- the inner discourse! I remembered reading an article of NSF - the National Science Foundation that the average person has "70,000 thoughts per day". On an average, an average person therefore could have 30-50 thoughts per minute hovering around the mind. The eminent Indian -American author and alternative medicine advocate **Dr Deepak Chopra (*****)** also endorsed such view.

What a fascinating info but how much of such thoughts we are storing it? How many of such thoughts are subsequently getting executed as we move forward? Or is it that most of these subsequently gets evaporated? May be with the rapid progress of human civilisation in the emerging digital world some innovation would happen which would enable tracking such data of our mind through research.

Sitting in the craft, I was sure that my mind surely had exceeded the figure of possible number of thoughts per minute in my brain as told by experts as obviously the mind was swamped with numerous thoughts on the sensitive subject. While keeping the tip of advises of my three bosses, my mind also had enough of homework during those three hours flight on possible strategies and approaches one should have while facing the turbulence from the local union. Bit of excitement, uncertainties, anxiety, tension, personal safety etc dominated the mind but I could hear the whisper from within: "hey buddy - it's an opportunity to show case your calibre - come on buddy- embrace it".

For safety and security reasons, I did not inform the local management about my place of accommodation as I never wanted the union to know about it. With the help of the branch manager, the next day morning I could organise meeting with the representatives of the local union in a neutral venue. First few hours obviously was an effort on the local union representatives part to exhibit their strength and rigidity. At times, few smarty amongst them pretended to be losing their patience and temparament. To show their toughness they did not accept my invitation of having lunch together. In the afternoon session almost same trend continued. Our reasoning, requests, logic etc had no impact whatsoever on them.

To calm them down, my strategy was to extend patience hearing and drag the issue for bit longer. Idea was to see if that slowed down their pace and I had to pretend to be extremely calm under pressure. Difficult but possible as one needs to have psychological preparedness. One of my key objective was to identify and pick up max 2-3 sensible guys amongst the agitating team and try to influence them at least to listen to us.

The constant communication with my bosses at the head quarter gave me a sense that we won't have to be rigid in our stance but innovate ways to resolve the impasse as we can't afford to take a hit on the dipping an revenue. The second day we kept on rallying around our respective viewpoints but there was little change in their body language from being rouge type to a slightly better body language. The fact that a responsible company executive came all the way from delhi perhaps gave them a feeling of being heard. Their slight change of attitude on the second day gave me a sense of increased confidence. Harping on my large organisation's contribution to social causes, contribution in bringing comforts to crores of people through their medicinal and other health care products, the company's values, principles in driving businesses, I was trying to keep them engaged and also create bit impact on their mind. Hardly the ice of their mind melted but it served the purpose of continuity of dialogue and bought us more time.

There had been umpteen number of cases where our organisation had taken tough stand against recalcitrant employees. Discipline had always been priority. But why suddenly the dilemma prevailed on my mind after listening to the key advise of my senior leadership team?

An interesting rather unusual advise was also there from leadership team to see our tough stance should not invite fresh trouble resulting to loss of revenues and market share. Was it a shift in our philosophy to deal with core values? Would it be a reason that our market research team few weeks back shared their findings that our main competitor, a regional player of South zone and more importantly in the state of Kerala was surging ahead with lot of new products and better margins to channel partners to augment the revenue. The indication was that this competitor would breathe on our shoulder shortly and if we don't deal with them strategically, we might possibly loose our market leadership. So, the frame of mind of the top leaders were understandable.

But how would one be expected to deal with dichotomy in a sensible subject on core values? The evasive mind faced the greatest challenge! On one hand tasks demands bit flexibility while dealing with the tasks, and on the other hand the mind says - "how can you do it by compromising with your principles?".

It's a task of conflict- resolution of mind and what would drive you to come out of the ambiguous mind? My mind suddenly took me to our management day's subject of psychology and relevance of 'flanker task' concept. I was tending to think of selective attention or rather which stimuli was capturing central part of mind and was tending to ignore many other stimuli hovering around the brain. The objective of the task, three superior bosses guidance, important views shared on shareholders expectations of better returns, competitors possible surging ahead of us, led me to brainstorming too and ultimately pushed me in getting response from within that 'go to the task route' amidst influence of "go - no go the task" and that was primarily due to my past learning of dealing with core values in the MNC.

That brings us to look at the views of some experts on 'go – no go' concept. – mentioned below.

"The Go – No Go"

The Dilemma – Value of the Values

Focus point:

The go/no - go is a cognitive task aimed at determining the ability of an individual to inhibit a response deemed inappropriate. Go/no go procedure involves psychological experiments, responding to questionnaire aimed at seeking response through specific tests which one can do even in their browser. The application of go/no go method to the lexical decision task was initiated by Gordon and Caramazza (******). Their belief was that this model produced better performance and data were less noisy. Lot of research on this subject was in place. There are contradictory views too.

During our dilemma specially on dealing with ethical issues, a conflict between alternatives that is visible, might lead us to compromise the laid down ethical principle while picking up one of the available alternatives. Such dilemma puts the mind to strong test since the individual has to pick up one out of the alternatives available. Mind might put us to a question that am I sacrificing the principle that I have been trained for so long?

While I asked views of some of the successful leaders, they came up with their own versions but the common point echoed which I could hear was -

"Believe in your confidence and ability as a leader. Rely on your sixth sense – rely on your guts And decision you would take, mostly would be right always".

Next two days both the side met couple of times to find out possible avenues to resolve the conflicting situations. Both the side finally realized that amicable solutions perhaps was beneficial for both the side. We agreed not to take stern action against the erring field executives. But written undertakings from such individuals were obtained requesting management to provide them with one more opportunity to work and written assurances were given expressing better performances and productivity from them. The union guys agreed to withdraw the agitational activities and assured co – operation. They agreed with our views that performance should be the key in justifying their role to support the organizational growth specially when competition was breathing on our shoulders.

The dead lock was over. The appreciation poured in. The task was accomplished but sitting in the craft, I did realize that there seems to be perpetually some iota of unhappiness prevailing still deep in my heart which was mainly due to my conflicting thought process in interpreting the values of the Core Values. What could be the possible reasons of such feelings?

- Was it due to my uncompromising personality traits as somewhere we as an organization could not exhibit the resilience in taking toughest call in sticking to our earlier toughest stand we took?
- Was it that my management grooming on such subject was contrary to what principle we followed here to achieve the goal? In other words, was it not bit compromise for the sake

of revenue? Was it not contrary to our "uncompromising" decision making stance we took in my previous organization at the MNC?

- Was it a realisation that learning or theories in corporate world is not written on the rock?
- Was it an issue in getting adopted to a new culture or guiding principles in dealing with Core Values based on organization's overall market leadership strategy including its focus on revenue?
- Was it that metamorphosis within me was transforming in getting in to my altered or renewed stride?

I suddenly could recall the faces of three of my stalwarts and their key concern on potential threat of losing our revenue, market share to competition etc. The importance of how should we hold on to our number one position in the market and revenue growth in the state of Kerala was the key focus. How would we manage the complexities with the external forums was our skill set – our responsibility? The messages were loud and clear.

While jubilation was kissing my mind definitely as we could resolve the impasse, but happiness in my mind perhaps was missing. The fatigued mind sitting in the window seat of the craft while returning to my head quarter had so many questions or dilemma:

1. Did I had to compromise in my own ethical standard in resolving the issues?
2. Or was it that perhaps what I did was best for the business interest?
3. Should we start perceiving that Core Values are not written in the rock?
4. Should we perceive that Values should be flexible to meet business and revenue objective?
5. Should I scrap my learning on core values of previous organization that Core Values were non - negotiable? Instead,

being professional, being hired to focus on key results areas (KRAs), one has to keep on adopting to situations while dealing with important subject like Core Values?

Was it a practical learning that in the changing business scenario customer is the prime? If your customer find your products and services were valuable and there were uninterrupted supply of your products amidst quality services, they will become mouthpieces of your products. They have the power to make or break your products. How the leadership team of that company was going to manage or handle the deviation from the Core Values by your own employees perhaps would be considered as your internal issue and you better deal with it.

That took me to recall the quote of **Scott Cook (*****)** who said:

"A brand is no longer what we tell the consumer it is – What consumer tell each other, it is".

Revenue is key – profit is motto – stake holders and various investors would watch on our capability to maximise return on their investments! Interesting learning indeed! You may ponder on thousand points but ultimately the fact remains that ' organization is larger than individual '.

Let's realize that we all have to deal with conflicting situations while handling business complexities and simultaneously be conscious about the spirit of Core Values while resolving issues. Tough tasks indeed. Individual's desire to strategize while adopting the best options or best possible opportunities that comes in front of us to resolve issues might reveal our personality, our character, our principle, our personal value system.

It's important to keep in mind our own values and the values of the Corporations which at times might not be identical. Our own values are instrumental while we move forward in pursuing our career. Amidst such dichotomy, perhaps the prospect of successful professional career, success that we all are chasing after, our beliefs need to be collaborative in line with the Values of the Organizations. That ultimately helps us in resolving personal dilemmas. Experts says that final decisions that are being taken are also anchored by our characteristics, principles, beliefs which triggers from our Values that is sitting in the central place of our subconscious mind.

To conclude, I thought of remembering relevant quote of **Beau Taplin (******)** in his 'Marching Heart':

"I think the beating in our hearts,

Was put there to remind us,

That even when we feel alone in the world,

a part of us marches on.

That even at our lowest we carry

Something inside us,

That we can learn on and turn to.

That even when we have no one else,

We always have ourselves".

"I fly with my cage – let the mind take me to a wonderland".

While returning back from cochin, I was staring through the craft's window at the milky white clouds amidst the sunny afternoon's pleasing blue sky, suddenly I was feeling sleepy amidst talking to myself that would those cumulus clouds which are puffy whites in patches forming shapes of cotton balls might have answer to my curiosities as they are floating in the thirty thousand feet height above the altitude? The most complex issue of the company has been resolved but why I am still unhappy? isn't it strange? What could be the possible reasons of my unhappiness prevailing inside me?

A crazy wish kissed my mind. It whispered in my ears that let the divine power bless me in gaining power with two powerful wings on my back and inspire me to dive through the tiny window of the craft to the divinity above the lovely visible clouds to seek answers why the mind is still not happy even after apparently achieving some complex goals?

The subconscious mind pecked my pair of eyes in my oblivious sleep. I could recall the fascinating poem of **Najib Manalai (****)** – the poet from Afghanistan and title of the poem was **"In The Plane"**:

"White and blue/blue and white,

With some distant memories of green,

I contemplate from above

The cotton – like chaos of the

empty skies.

Too small an opening, the window,

Prevents me from knowing more,

I fly with my cage".

Learning scenario – From this leading FMCG - an Indian multinational:

Yes - core values are key. But equally important is business, revenue, market share, stakeholders value creation keeping eye on competition. Grow the business phenomenally. Become a force to reckon with. And simultaneously create awareness on value of Value

Business objectives may lead you to deal with conflicting situations diplomatically!

Key take home - Well, when you hang on to straws in such confluence situations, you may resolve the toughest conflicting situations but may be with an iota of compromise somewhere in the belief systems. You may be lauded by the organization. But would such compromise, even if it was insignificant, lead you to shed a few drops of tears in the midst of rain without being noticed by others?

What if you could guide the mind in such complex tasks?

Learning episode 3

From the Promoter driven leading Infrastructure sector –

A study of the huge number of Indian business house would reveal that large percentage of such business houses are either family run or promoter driven. Many of such houses are listed entities in the stock market and many of them have significant presence globally. A report some time back from 'Credit Suisse' (*****) reflected that India holds the third position globally in terms of family- driven organisation. Encouraging – isn't it?

Success of many of such promoter driven organizations perhaps would be their aspirations in building successful organizations where inter – alia they emphasised on the importance of basic values. Most of such houses believed strongly that if the foundation of the organizations are based on effective Core Values then business would be sustainable. And therefore, the cohesive culture gradually gets build where professionals enthusiastically tries to get aligned with the philosophy and value system of the organizations as they find similarity of their value system with that of organizations.

Having shared the interesting exposures on Core Values and how it was addressed by one of the best global giant in the pharmaceuticals and health care organization (MNC) and also by one of the best-in-class Indian multinational Corporates, it would now be equally interesting to share the learning from a Promoter driven Indian conglomerate where the professionals played key role but promoters were also involved in the business.

By virtue of my role in the leadership arena and by virtue of working with the top management of each of these organisations and that too more than a decade in each of those establishments, enlightened my knowledge on such a sensitive subject – the Core Values.

While predominantly this organization was in the infrastructure sector, they gradually could spread their wings in to diverse sectors. The organization started enjoying the rapid growth both in terms of volume and value of businesses and naturally we saw a huge growth in manpower numbers too.

Being diverse organization with leaders coming from varied background, it was felt that Core Values could be a common glue in holding each one of those diverse business entities in to one thread. The promoters took the initiative through the professionals in ensuring that values are defined and articulated. Learning was clear – the top management has to hold the rein of building culture and values, nurture it constantly while encouraging leadership team members to see that values were percolating down the line.

The debatable episode centring around Core Values:

Usually the leadership team is sensible in dealing with misconducts. It encourages the Human Resource department to follow the process in such case. Two interesting observations: 1) usually being driven by knowledge workers, such sort of so called misconducts etc hardly takes place 2) the mind - set of the top leaders including the promoter had been more to rely on counselling the erring employees, provide opportunities to its people to correct themselves.

In this interesting case, one of the Business leader along with the Head of Human resources confronted a middle management level guy named Ritesh who was found to be involved in a case of accepting bribe. Ritesh the family man had two kids and was staying in a rented house. He had applied for some bank loan as they were aspiring for a small ownership flat. Ritesh had been in the organization for more than seven years. He was professionally qualified. He though was not reckoned as a high performer but was considered as a stable guy who knew his job.

The process of domestic enquiry was followed and the charges were proved. The issue was sensitive. It had a linkage with 'integrity' which incidentally was one of the Core Values of the company. The authority took the firm step of terminating the employee. Most unfortunate but the hidden objective was to send silent message across that company would not compromise with the Core Values. Ritesh's appeal to extend him a lighter punishment was not accepted by the management. Dismissal decision was maintained.

Unique learning of an approach on Core Values – Is it written on the rock?

It was almost two years since it happened and a lot of water had gone under the bridge when one fine morning Ritesh with an appeal met the VC and explained:

1. The toughest hardship he and his family with two young kids were facing
2. The kind of efforts he made in securing alternate job which did not materialise
3. He shared how he tried even in venturing in to a small trading business which got flopped.
4. how his family had pulled him up for his conduct?
5. How terribly he had been repenting for his wrong doing and how he picked up the lessons of life under such circumstances?
6. And of course the most emotional point that how frustration was seizing the family specially for the two innocent kids. Ritesh continued his appeal to the company's Vice Chairman describing him as great human being who had shaped careers of thousands of people by providing opportunity. He was giving all sort of assurances including written assurance of perfect conduct.

VC during our discussions wanted my views on such appeal etc. Being the torch bearer or rather protagonist of the company's Core Values, I had no hesitation of ruling out accepting such appeal. I went on to highlight what sort of wrong message it would send across organization. How such consideration on our part might move around the corridor impacting discipline, morale of the performing people and ultimately business!

The facial expressions of my VC reflected clearly that he was not surprised with my views! We debated on the issue of being sympathetic. Views were getting exchanged but what charmed me was his strategic outlook in the larger context of not only building organizations but what kind of larger role or mentality we all need to possess while dealing with values centring around people issue.

Crux of his viewpoints were as follows:

i. Beside building organization, how important it was to be a human in your approach.

ii. Discipline is core but we have role in building society too through shaping life of people. Termination is important but what would happen to the socio – economic situation of the family members specially to the two young kids of the erring employee who were not at fault? Are we not pushing such family in to deeper trouble? Would not such issue bring more challenges to our socio – economic system?

iii. Sheer punishment would not serve the objective. We as employer also need to shoulder perhaps the role of 'social reformer and make efforts in correcting mind of erring employee(s)'.

iv. Measure the mentality rather psychology of mind of those erring employees as to are they repenting for their misconduct and ready to rectify his/ her mentality? Then do give them a chance to come back to organization as such guys could be more conscious and productive. But keep a watch on such guys for the first few months. Organization would achieve many folded advantages.

What an unique rather wise learning it was. Such simple but impactful philosophical idea reminded me of the famous Latin phrase which came from French philosopher **Rene Descartes (****)** that "I think and therefore I am". Once one is in thinking mode, then one would be in a position to manipulate information to form concepts, to reason and to come out with ideal decisions.

The classic example of reforming human minds

Chairman of one of the organization I had worked with, beside being an eminent Industrialist was a great contributor of reforming human minds. Being a great story teller, he had unique style of influencing leaders whenever they had challenges in dealing with complex people problem. His illustrations through various motivational stories were mostly based on great characters from our mythology. He use to emphasise on the leaders developing the skill of influencing erring employees through persuasion.

In one of the interesting case, we were debating on should we take a tough stand on one of the key member of the business team as the guy allegedly were involved in some controversial business transactions? While few of us were advocating termination of the guy based on company's ethics policy, he obviously supported the stand but shared an interesting story from our mythology and wanted us to ponder on our decision before actioning it.

The gist of the story was so relevant that it compelled us to take a pause and review our decision. It was so apt for the leaders who were to deal with all sorts of people. Angulimala's story had created so much impact that it is often referred to in erudite discussions where focus gets in to cases of transforming human mind, justice and rehabilitation. Ahimska's becoming known or named as Angulimala (the finger necklace), the infamous killer was interesting. Subsequently, the turn of significant events transformed him into a important figure in Buddhism. For the leaders from any discipline, specially the management practitioners, his story was an inspiring lesson that everyone can change their life for the better, even the least likely people. His was a case of sudden transformation from a vicious killer to an enlightened disciple.

The story had essence of best of the management and leadership lessons. The usual competition amongst students or Sisyas in the Ashram – a kind of Gurukul where Ahismska, the handsome, intelligent and one of the most promising student became target of the co- students where jealousy, hatred led to brilliant Ahismka's getting trapped in the ploy resulting in his Guru's getting irked. The usual biased decision of Guru compelled Ahimska to move to dense forest in order to achieve the dreadful task of bringing 1000 human fingers from 1000 individuals – a task which Guru thought could not be accomplished and therefore, Ahimska won't be able to complete his siksha and attain status of being a monk. Once he fails to achieve his toughest task, he would be compelled to embrace the highest frustration of his life and that perhaps could be the best revenge or punishment to have.

The story touched upon the example of highest respect of the disciple to his mentor cum Guru. It highlighted the highest spirit of the mentee to accomplish the task given even though the task itself was dreadful. A determined Ahimska could seize his victims passing through the forest roads and had manage to get 999 fingers, almost the quota of fingers demanded by his Guru. Incidentally, he became infamous for his notorious activity. For the smooth counting of the fingers, he stringed the fingers on a thread and most interestingly he use to wear them as sacrificial thread. It looked like he was wearing 'necklace of fingers'. This was the key reason of him being known as "Angulimala"

Subsequently, the story focussed on his mother's emotion where mother could overlook the heinous crime of son. Fearing his son's life in danger, she could manage to reach Angulimala to save and protect from the kings intent of hunting him down to punish. The height of commitment to achieve Guru's given task, Angulimala for a moment thought of making her mother as the 1000th victim so that he could become a monk and subsequently attain 'Abhinna', a miraculous power.

Buddha through his meditative mind could foresee that once Angulimala slains his mother, he would not be able to be a monk as matricide in Buddhism would be one of the worst crime. Buddha arrived on the spot. Angulimala changed his mind. Instead of killing his mother, he chooses to kill Buddha and started chasing Buddha. Buddha uses his super natural power where finally a bewildered Angulimala realised that his efforts would be futile, surrendered to Buddha to take advise and guidance. From Budddha, he could learn a lot and declared himself converted, vows to cease his life as a brigand and joined the Buddhist monastic order.

The key idea:

Classic story of Angulimala is one of the most well- known story not only in our country but across many countries. The story is an example of the compassion and supernatural accomplishments. It is also a testimony to the capabilities of a great mentor or teacher. It replicates the inspiring, influencing and healing power of a teacher. The story is an example that misled, erring people, can come back to right path once the realization happens.

Let's quote the view point of David Loy (****), the eminent ethics scholar. He felt that according to Buddhist ethics, the wrong doers should be punished with sole objective of reforming their characters. Since Angulimala had already gone through the process of reforming himself, why would there be further punishments? Loy however, observed flaw in the story since it did not include any form of transformative justice. Citing logic of capital punishment, scholar Damien Horigan (****) felt that prime theme of the story was focussed on rehabilitation.

The British – born Theravadamonk Ajahn Khemadhammo (****) founded Angulimala, a Buddhist prison Chaplaincy organization in UK. Recognised by the British governments, this organization is encouraged to counselling services and spread meditation practises for the British prisoners throughout England, Wales and Scotland. The organization's philosophy refers to the power of transformation where Angulimala's story ignites the minds. They felt that lesson

from Angulimala story preaches the possibility of enlightenment may get ignited in the most complex circumstances as people can navigate themselves to change and can be highly influenced through persuasion skills.

Angulimala's legend has received considerable attention and 'take away' for us, especially for the practitioners of people is immense. The philosophy of reforming the mind of an erring employees and subsequently helping them to rehabilitation would make this world a great place to live in. But such philosophical thinking can happen once we decide to think to move away from our set practises and beliefs.

The ancient Greek philosopher Socrates (***) felt that Philosophical thinking begins at the moment we stop taking things for granted, marvel at them and ask questions about them. It was said that the difference between Socrates and his friends were that his friends were content with limited and often incoherent ideas, whereas Socrates was inspired by wonder to investigate further. Socrates felt that beginning of philosophy is wonder; Much of the philosophical thinking is concerned with examining the things that we often take as granted.

Was it that I was unable to think beyond the conventional thought process of "no mercy to Ritesh because he was found involved in misconduct"? Was it that we had limitations in our thought process in moving beyond traditional corporate ideas of 'zero tolerance' on integrity or other serious misconducts?

The Vice Chairman in Ritesh's case and the Chairman's Angulimala example just provoked us to think beyond the canvas. Perhaps we never thought of thinking beyond the rationale that policies and processes are not written in the rock. Life's worth is also to add value by reforming or transforming erring human minds. To be philosophical is to stay detached and thoughtful in the face of a complex or tough situation.

Learning scenario – From this promoter driven large infrastructure company

Your ethos are your driving forces in building business. Beside profit, we need to be conscious about social order – social structure. Driving organization necessitates you to ponder on "I think and therefore I am ". We need to be different.

Learning here has been that wrong doers should be punished. But do not be rigid in losing an opportunity of reforming one's mind – conduct. If that difficult task can be achieved then we achieve larger objective too.

Key lesson? Value of Values are infinite!!

Episode 4.

"Leading self" - dichotomy in tackling what comes first? The business strategy? Re - looking in to the Vision? Reframing the Core Values? Revitalise or tinkering the Business Model? Restructuring the Organization structure?

Fascinating story of turning around an Organization, plagued with all such complexities. From one of the European Country -

Here is an interesting story of a relatively smaller organization from the financial sector of one of the European country – An exciting episode of an young, dynamic CEO's prioritising the task while taking over the challenging but exciting assignment of turning around the company.

It was about leadership dynamics of Christian K (CK) - a professional from Germany. CK had the distinction of contributing to some of the best-in-class companies across Europe. He was considered to be a successful leader predominantly in the financial sector and then he decided to move away from the specialist role to generalist role and accepted one of the most challenging, complex and exciting offer of taking over the role of a CEO in driving and leading a company immersed with all sort of predicament.

And the story is the challenge of prioritising the tasks, and bring the institution back to revenue track.

Being good friend's over a period of time, CK and I use to keep on exchanging interesting views on Organization Development strategies, People perspective, Performance orientation culture, designing career aspiration plan of potential performers, Culture building. Interestingly, we also use to discuss on our common interest on sports and that too mainly soccer.

My curiosity therefore, was high to learn from CK the strategies that brought results. It was unique learning on a 'Sunny Sunday' when we agreed to have good chat focussing on leadership style in doing things differently which brought him the success. Let's highlight the salient points emerged out of the conversation:

MSD – So, Dear **CK** – Compliment for leading your organization successfully but I am more keen to know what prompted you to leave a cosy, secured, well paid job in a leading organization and accept a challenging, complex task of leading an unstable organization plagued with all kind of complexities as CEO?

CK – With a smile - paused a little to introspect......

The points you raised on what prompted me to look for changes while accepting this new assignment were so true. From the core of my heart I was realising that I was becoming complacent. Being in a well - settled role for quite some time, I got in to a 'Comfort zone' for last few years. Was it killing my passion, my drive? My attitude of resilience was drying up. Challenges appeared to be well under control – no more anxiety. The excitement of creating something new and thereby adding value was descending. My conscience was whispering in my ears that it's high time CK that you move out of your comfort zone – take challenge – create your own excitement and add value to yourself and to your new but challenging tasks. You have huge time left to hang up your gloves! It was a kind of 'self – talk'. 'Dialogues with self" which finally facilitated in my decision making process and brought me here!

MSD – You are so true. I can imagine the different stages your mind had gone through and I was recalling the views of the experts from the field of psychology. Let me share with you an insight I got on this key subject and perhaps it would help you to co-relate such theories with what your mind passed through.

Let's remember this:

A comfort zone can be described as ' a psychological state in which things feel familiar to a person and they are at ease and in control of their environment, experiencing low levels of anxiety and stress. Obviously, stepping out of comfort zone will generate stress to a certain extent. But still many of us do it. Why?

In real life, it is important to becoming a better- rounded person because by 1) pushing ourselves from comfort zone, we can untap knowledge and resources from our stores because our knowledge and ability could be much higher then we think. 2) Risks are growth experiences too and increases our knowledge. 3) Letting your comfort dictate your experience in no way to live. 4) Setting for mediocrity is an incredibly high price you pay for the feeling of relative safety. 5) The moment you move out of the comfort zone, you are expanding and diversifying your comfort zone.

Over a century ago, noted psychologist Robert Yerkes (****) told of a behavioural space wherein in order to maximize the performance, humans must reach stress levels that are higher than normal. References are from 'Array Behavioural Care' (****) – Chicago.

Let's look at from neuroplasticity angel – reference Palm Health (*****)- Missouri. From Neuroplasticity point of view, the other interesting analogue would be to learn our brain's ability to reorganize and form new connections and pathways between its cells in response to learning of new experiences. Thus, creating as many new pathways between neurons as possible – increasing neuroplasticity – helps brain to stays sharp and focussed. Stepping out of comfort zone with unfamiliar activities is what triggers the rewiring of our brain,

which is a concept known as neuroplasticity. Luckily, improving our own neuroplasticity is something we have control.

CK – Appreciate! Yes – I can now corelate it easily. The knowledge that you shared is apt and would help me to also guide my leadership team.

Well, MSD - It had been wonderful so far. Last three years challenges vis a vis the opportunities have ignited my passion. I could strongly realize that such challenging tasks had put me to the acid test of my leadership skill and again, I started feeling the 'fire under my belly'!

You know - in last three years, we have tasted some success but we also have realized that we are yet to accomplish many more. The focus would be there to achieve those too.

But before I narrate the points you wanted me to share, it's important to paint the canvas of real hurdles that welcomed me while I took over. Gaining confidence of the regulators, ensuring stake holder's value creation, focussing on performance oriented culture that too in an organization where cross cultural team from seven different countries had to be tackled. Besides, re - positioning the brand to gain back customers confidence, tinkering the business model and emphasising on Digital intervention in diversifying new businesses were amongst key challenges. I could observe in short time that Vision and Core Values that you were talking about was claimed to be existing in the organization. But it was merely present in the posters and notice boards and was not getting demonstrated in most of the employees aptitude and attitude.

MSD – Interesting indeed! My focus therefore, is to learn from you very specifics. During our discussions sometime back on your views on Vision and Core Values, you spoke about your unconventional approach to vision and core values while taking over the challenging assignment. We know ultimately your strategy or rather style of leadership brought results too. Would you like to elaborate on this important aspect?

CK – Yes, I acknowledge that Vision and Core Values are very important to focus while taking over assignment in a new company.

But.... a pause..... with a smile again CK continued.

CK – Look, unfortunately, I did not have the luxury of time. Impatient stake holders were breathing on my shoulder. The canvas I was greeted with was extremely challenging, I was clear that conventional way of leading won't bring result. Rather, I was clear in my conviction that my purpose should be to look at the challenges from a variety of lenses and frames. Because each one illuminates more of the situations and gives you deeper insights. I remembered one of quote from a great leader that: "In leadership, character is more important that strategy".

Interestingly, with the changing scenario in the market place, we have been shifting our goalpost too. Because market trends and market dynamics should determine our objectives. Therefore, the unique learning that we realized was that our leadership style, or creating Vision and Core Values etc should not be conventional and neither it should be written on the rock. Rather these are to be aligned with market behaviour based on customer centricity. It is clearly situation based.

MSD – Interesting indeed! We have seen leaders taking over challenging assignment spend their energy in creating business model and simultaneously setting up Vision and Core Values so that the entire organization is aligned. In your case, you seemed to be doing it differently. Thought provoking but I am getting more keen to understand what drove you?

CK – I respect the trend or Industry practise that you are talking about. But to me the Vision and Core Values appeared to be a fudgy statement given the serious challenges I was greeted with from the first day – first hour. The dip in the revenue. The threat to our survival.

So, I felt spending energy in trying to create and drive Vision and Core Values at that point of time was not relevant. Rather, traits of leading from front, setting examples with actions, showing guts, calling spade a spade in dealing with unfavourable situations in initial team meetings, indomitability in driving revenues and reduce cost and expenses simultaneously from the very beginning at that stage was more relevant and practical. People had to acclimatize in our calling spade a spade and made to belief that either we perform together or perish together! Therefore, they would be observing your actions on the floor and market place rather than listening to advises, management jargons on importance of values.

MSD – Encouraging indeed to hear such philosophy. So, what were the strategic steps you drove home in transforming the company and did you finally touched upon and communicated the company's Vision and Core Values, as I am keen to understand that?

A pause ...CK's face portrayed a philosophical and introspective mode.

CK – Well, if I glance through the interventions that we followed, I could possibly summarise them through the following steps:

STEP 1

Setting perspective

- Listen to investor's concern/expectations/advises
- Meet the key customers/governance forums, external – seek view points
- Reach out to employees

STEP 2

Lead by example

- Walk - the - talk
- Focus on performance rather revenues
- Demonstrate how to create values in each step -
- Polite but firm in seeking results

STEP 3

Calibrating culture

- Don't overstate - but share serious concern/challenges
- Culture of encouraging - not to hide weaknesses but bring it to the table

- Identify people who may compliment your skill or weaknesses

STEP 4

Owning up

- Encourage ownership & empowerment
- Encourage tabling wrong decisions to resolve it together
- Encourage removing extra layers in the hierarchy

STEP 5

Touching Core Values skilfully

- Governance - internal or external - no deviation
- Zero tolerance on integrity, underperformance, indifferent attitude - (example? one rotten apple in a basket of good apples would impact good ones).

STEP 6

Inching towards vision and core values

- Results happening by this time -
- People appreciating the changes/transformation processes
- That enabled us to drive the larger Goal
- It became easy now to share our Vision and framing the Core Values as by this time most of the people started believing in us and believing in themselves as results started coming in.

Therefore, MSD – you would appreciate that based on toughest situations when I took over, I was clear that not to impose or spend energy in Creating Vision and Core Values through posters, messages, displays in notice boards, communication slides etc which any leader would prefer doing. I wanted to do it differently.

Over a period of first 3-4 quarters of financial year, people observed our action, our intentions carefully. They could gradually realize the logic of our actions and decisions even though some of such actions by us might not have been pleasant. But the people also knew that the ship we together were sailing had been going through roughest climate. It's exciting to watch Titanic movie in the movie hall but not in real life. No one would like to imagine being in such a ship to be greeted with that sort of fate!

Perhaps somewhere deep in their heart they also wanted to be driven by a reliable navigator to save the ship they were sailing from being capsized – that's the human mind!!

I realize that if I start believing myself as smart, people can be smarter. I believed in the theory of leader's needs to be effective mentor and that is more important rather than finding fault unnecessarily with your people. People started feeling happy with the revenue getting back to track. New businesses started happening. Investors and Governance team tending to believe in our strategies and efforts. And therefore, people started getting used to our "walk- the – talk" in driving home strong messages on our motives and objectives which included emphasising on our Value system too. Not sure, but I guess by that time they realized that the CEO is a no – nonsense guy! Such image perhaps also was important at that point of time.

Hence, I was talking about unconventional way of driving Vision and Core Values unlike others. Well, having said so, I guess, your point on some leader's focussing on Vision and Core Values in the beginning might be right and relevant as the situations they might have got while taking over the company might have been different. But mine was unique!

A point to ponder:

Like most of us, I used to believe upon the strategy of developing Core Values during the early part of the company's history or reviewing the Core Values once the CEO takes over the responsibility. I could recall the write ups in Harvard Business Review column too which supported such views and let's look at them in the below noted notes.

Focus point:

In one of the Harvard Business Review magazine, I came across an interesting point, when Tony Hsieh (****), founder of Zappos, was asked what he would do differently if he could restart his company from scratch. He without hesitation uttered that: "If I could go back and do Zappos all over again, I would actually come up with our values from day one".

But the learning story from CK made us to think differently. He followed the unconventional method of dealing with business issues, challenges rather than initially spending time and energy in setting Vision and Core Values. When results started happening through 'change management initiatives' around 9 – 12 months of time of CK's taking over, it became easier for CK and his leadership to communicate thereafter about business Vision and Core Values as interestingly, people started believing in themselves as well as the leadership of CK and his key team. So, the trust which disappeared in view of the leadership scenario of the past, started appearing again.

Was it that during earlier management's time, people inclined to get aligned with the change initiatives? Was it that they had lost the trust factor on their leaders? In psychology, trust is believing that a person who is trusted will do what is expected. According to Eric Erikson (****), the eminent psychoanalyst, development of basic trust is the first step of psychological development occurring, or failing during initial phase. Was it that in CK's case, positive changes in company's performance was enabling the trust factor to come back again?

Similarly, mistrust which was prevalent in the organization, happens from valid response to feeling abandoned, failure in keeping commitment or betrayed. Sometime mistrust plays a dominant role in people's life. Past disappointments before CK era might be at the root of the issue. Pervasive feelings of mistrust can negatively impact a person's life. This can result in anger, anxiety, or self- doubt. Good news for us is psychologists believe that fortunately people can relearnt trust. From 'GoodTherapy' (*****).

Therefore, was it that past leadership's failure to drive home revenues, performance, positive culture had impacted the mind of people with 'mistrust'?

Each story could be different – Each circumstances could be unique. There can't be any laid down formulae that you can adopt while deciding in which stage of business one should emphasise in creating Vision or Core Values.

As leader, we are to evaluate the situations from different lenses and frames – review it and then drive towards the right perspectives.

2

OLD WAYS WON'T OPEN NEW DOORS

Culture predominantly stems out of Core Values. However, there could be gap between ideal and prevalent culture in the organization.

It's about a 'true story' of how the newly joined CEO of a century old bit orthodox brand, through his dynamic leadership influenced the culture during the journey of transformation.

The learning also has been about organization's readiness to accept the painful journey while striving for cultural changes.

Easier said than done!

Culture trumps strategy every time-

- **Towards the journey of attaining transformed leadership –**

"Change almost never fails because it's too early. It almost fails because it's too late" – Seth Godin

What a relevant idea from Godin!!

Let's glance through the most exciting stories of mid- nineties of a leading FMCG giant - Durbs. It's a classic case of an apparently orthodox 'Promoter driven' large organization's daring to transform their 102 years old organization to newer heights!

It was first time in their history of Durbs – the family driven 102 years organization when they aspired to bring in a professional top notch CEO in spite of presence of the families the third generation young stars who were well nurtured, formally educated from best of global management institutes and were capable too to lead any institution. But then the family counsel must have had more reasons coupled with wisdom to attract one of the best CEO available at that point of time from best – in – class MNC of the FMCG sector. We will talk about this interesting story in the subsequent paragraphs.

Well, before sharing the most interesting story of transforming Durbs, which in subsequent years became one of the best–in–class FMCG company of the country, I was getting the provocation to briefly touch upon almost a similar story from **Bill Marriott (****), the Executive Chairman of Marriott group** across geographies about his toughest decision of choosing the first Non - family CEO for the first time in the history of the company.

Bill Marriott shared how he was chosen over a professional executive VP whom everyone thought would move as CEO. Under Bill's able leadership, the group moved pretty fast and became a force to reckon with in the Industry. When Bill Marriott was 57, leading the business steadily, he suffered a heart attack. Uncertainties prevailed in this giant global family driven business. But Bill bounced back to business leading it across 73 countries with revenue steadily moving up. That was the time Bill started thinking about succession planning.

Marriott had four children and was sure that one of them from the family would move to the coveted role of CEO. Eyes were on John Marriot who was already doing well in the organization. John moved in to every part of business to gain exposure. The perception in the corporate corridor was that John would succeed Bill.

Interestingly, reaching closer to age of 80 years, Bill realised that it was not right fit – not for John, and not for the company. While rotating Bill in some challenging role to nurture and groom him for larger role,

Bill observed that John was performing but happiness was missing as some elements of the job might not have enthused John. But those elements of the job was essentially important to be a CEO. So, both father and son had meeting over dinner and they resolved amicably that John would not pursue the CEO's role.

Rightly Bill acknowledged that personally it was disappointing for both of them to agree to such decision on not offering John the CEO role. But then John was given equally challenging role of vice chairman of the board. He was also taken as CEO of JWM Family enterprises, a family trust that was founded by John.

And in the process, Bill brought in a top class litigator and nurtured him finally to a manager. Arne was taken through the head of litigation, then the heading the mergers and acquisition team. Post that, he was assigned CFO role. Subsequently, got exposure in people skill which according to Bill was a key trait in the hospitality sector.

Therefore, it was a well thought grooming of the successor of Bill who never believed in horse race\succession, be it from the family members or be it from the external world of professionals. Bill believed that it would have been disruptive and the person who loses inevitably would end up leaving the company. That was not acceptable too to Bill. What a great learning!

In the meantime, John also went up the ladder successfully and was enjoying driving what he wanted. It was a successful startegy of having John also in important key role.

And finally almost at the age of 80, Bill decided to make the transition official as Arne take over as the first professional CEO of the so long family led business. Bill shared that it was the most exciting moment for the family and the entire organization.

(taken from HBR**)**

Let's come back to our intended sharing of one of the most exciting story from Durbs. While crucial decision was taken by the promoters to transform the organization during mid-nineties, most of the complex problem 'Durbs' had to tackle were attributed to its culture which in other word can be said that it was due to the reverence for the company's 102 – year history.

Operating in the Ayurveda based health care and family care product sector, 'Durbs' had been a popular name in the country. Most of its products were enjoying good market share. However, ideating new product development, penetrating to newer geographies, compounding the CAGR or revolutionising the ideas on maximising return on capital deployed, innovative strategies, ambitious vision, bringing best practises in every sphere of business was missing. Culture perhaps encouraged the people to be steadfast and therefore, mediocrity, job security was common feature. Unwritten philosophy emerged that once you are in a job, you may look up to your retirement age irrespective of your productivity but you have to show up every day and maintain peaceful environment in the workplace. Was it more of loyalty that used to be counted? Preference for employment of the loyalists' employees' family members was in place too. Attritions had never been a issue specially at the leadership level.

New entrants at leadership level, whenever inducted by promoters to infuse innovative ideas, painting larger pictures of growth, passion to pursue such ambitious growth could hardly perform or continue in absence of collaborative leadership culture, lack of support.

The sophisticated promoters family were as a bit orthodox in their approach to tackle the prevailing complacency for ages. May be, was it that consumers were happy with the quality of the products, profit though insignificant was happening and the brand Durbs became a trustworthy familiar name in the market. Well, perhaps that perception of market was wrong about the promoters avoiding initiating change management agenda specially when many organizations drove successfully such agenda post the opening up of Indian Economy during early nineties. In fact, the promoters being the top level entrepreneur were getting ready for the right timings to initiate the transformation initiatives amidst apprehension that prevalent culture could be hurdle in pushing the strategy to transform both business and organization.

Focus point:

That's where Dr Amantha Imber (****) rightly echoed in one of his column sharing – "creative destruction is the key difference between leadership and management". He rightly shared that – "its no longer about how an organization responds to change, rather it is about how an organization can predict and restructure for changes that are yet to happen. If organization wait until external changes happen before responding, it is likely that competitors that predicted the change are already extracting value from the market. With industry, products and technology lifecycles becoming shorter, the need for leaders who can cope with change, set direction and align and motivate people is increasing at unprecedented rates".

Keeping in mind the above, it's perhaps a co-incidence that the professionally qualified next generation of the promoters ambitious young stars started getting in to business. They with their mentors from the Promoter's family wanted to fuel the mindset of 'establishing urgency'. They were influenced by the strong belief that without pushing the agenda of 'urgent need for change', structural inertia can be insurmountable.

In addition to the above, the investors – the promoters developed conviction that the company was not capitalizing its potential grow manyfold. But unfortunately what Durbs promoters at that point of time did not recognize was that for all its benefits and blemishes, it was the legacy that they were carrying. So, the result or desire to change was eluding them. The Board and the promoter family decided to rope in one of the best global management consulting organization to not only chalk out the intervention plan, growth strategy etc but very wisely the consulting firm was given the mandate of not only to advise steps to transformation but to handhold and work with the leadership team during the change management process.

"And the journey began ...."

The key learning – Perhaps Promoters were confident that change was essential and it's high time that they must walk the talk. Rest of the things would fall in place simultaneously. They were convinced that prima - facie culture change was the top priority and together with the global top consulting firm a well thought road map was put in place.

Key idea:

John R. Katzenbach, Ilona and Caroline's (****) covering the write up on a magazine of Harvard Business Review on "Cultural Change that sticks" seemed to be apt in this interesting case study of Durbs.

The author felt that a strategy that is at odds with a company's culture is doomed. Culture trumps strategy every time. Interestingly

they shared that "we have known for a long time that it takes years to alter how people think, feel and behave, and even then, the difference may not be meaningful. When that's the case, an organization with an old powerful culture can devolve in to disaster. This has happened to many organizations across the globe. Happily, it was also possible that cultures do evolve over a period of time – sometimes slipping backward and sometimes progressing – and the best you can do is work with and within them, rather than fight them.

Therefore, Durbs promoters prioritizing the 'cultural change' through change management aspect was the wisest step in an environment where most of the workforce had reverence to 102 years old history and legacy. The promoters along with the new CEO worked out the strategic road map to bring transformation in all aspect. A well orchestrated action plan over period of time turned around the situation in bringing the desired result and it was a history which subsequently turned out to be an interesting case law in the corporate world.

The interventions were galore, time framed, exciting and result oriented. My purpose here is not to get in to all those aspects but maintain focus on the key point of this chapter – reform and realign the culture in line with strategic intent, transformation, leadership.

Strategic intent of exponential growth including aspirations to be a global player were articulated through adequate flow of communication. Steps were taken from being seen as an 'Ayurveda based company' to a premier health and family care product. Repositioning the brand image accordingly, Remaining focussed on existing strength too like quality assurance, research orientation (R & D), distribution channel. From one company and balance sheet, moving in to developing SBUs – multiple profit centres in line with new product category/segmentation. Expanding the R & D capability in line with such goal. Developing newer geographies, new channel partners. Building a Pan India image from 'one zone' based penetration. Revamping the marketing strategy including development of the brand building strategy – encouraged higher budget on marketing thrust including advertisement through

ATL and BTL (above the line and below the line) and ensure more visibility. Attracting vibrant sales and marketing professionals with a vigour to drive ambitious revenues. Dealing with mediocrity especially at leadership roles and replacing them by attracting talent from the best in class organisations. and therefore had enough of leaders to exhibit the few behaviours that matter most. Inevitably, significant changes began happening!

And most importantly, to put the final 'nail on the coffin of doubts', the significant decision of promoters taking back seat at a right moment after inducting a top notch CEO for the first time in the history of Durbs had send a strong signal across the organization about the intention of the promoters.

Breaking stereotypes leadership - 'destruct to construct' -

One of the most significant day around autumn at Durbs unfolded. Autumn, being the spring season witnesses falling of leaves and new leaves comes in!! Nature turns out to be little brown and drab. Many of us enjoy such change in the nature as fresh leaves are always soothing for the eyes. Like the change in the nature, would people draw inference to the beginning of the change of the 'laid back culture' in Durbs with the announcement of new CEO's stepping in?

Since last few days, the recently joined Director- Human Resources being reckoned as a successful senior leader in the Industry and his team was busy in planning the welcome and induction of the new CEO - Mr Neel K (NK), (camouflaged the name). It was for the first time in Durbs when the Managing Director from the promoters family decided to stay back and handed over the baton for the first time in the 102 years history to a professional. Came in NK, an IIM alumni and a successful top notch professional with best-in-class FMCG exposure including overseas assignments. He had impressive track record to lead and transform organizations and was being perceived as one of the 'Grandiose'.

The plan to send a Mercedes to NK's residence on the first day to his South Delhi his residence and then extend a grand welcome on his arrival at the factory -cum - head office got a jolt as such idea was nipped in the bud by NK himself much to the utter surprise and perhaps a bit of dejection of the leadership team who all were also bit excited to participate in the grand welcome of their top notch professional CEO. NK's idea in discarding such usual plan was simple but unusual. He felt sending car was unnecessary as he had own car and instead of wasting few hours in the elaborative welcome plan, together they must surge ahead with action from the very first hour. Was it a strong message from a change navigator from the first stroke? Well, more surprises were in store!!

With excitement galore, the head of HR, the security commander, few other key leaders were waiting in the security office near the entry gate at about 9 am a time which was conveyed to NK as beginning of the office working hour. Perhaps they wanted to receive NK at the entrance gate itself. After all it's the most prize attraction of talent for the organization. They were expecting the branded four wheeler of NK to hit the security gate. Guards were well prepared to welcome.

Much to the utter surprise of all, instead of arrival of the much talked about new leader in a classy Mercedes, a two wheeler, a Harley – Davidson buzzed in to the gate. Let's acknowledge that Harley Davidson was scarce in India during those days. A gorgeous leather jacket, a top class helmet with protective hand gloves, appeared a sturdy rider. Sitting on the dazzling two wheeler, the sturdy man whispered to the security guard to lift the guard rail but yes – not before introducing him as the newly appointed CEO. The baffled security guard before deciding to take advise of the security inspector, appeared to be mesmerized so much that he robotically opened the guard rail to allow entry of the two- wheeler. In tinkle of a sec the motorbike reached the main office gate which was some 150 meters from the security gate.

The most sought – after news of the morning of the CEO's arrival by a Harley – Davidson spread like a wild fire. The Director Human Resources and other key leaders rushed pretty fast to meet and greet NK at the office entrance. Apparently cool NK removed his gears after parking the Harley-Davidson. A measured smile from him was good enough for the assembled members that he was quite at ease and meant business from the first minute after entering the premises in the first but significant day. In no time the GM-operation arrived in view of

NK's specific advise and both of them together disappeared inside the plant. The bewildered HR Director and few other senior leaders decided to give up their ideas of welcoming and greeting. They moved back to their offices and one could imagine what all was happening in their guess work of such behaviour of the CEO on his first day!!

Was it not fascinating? Was it not an out of box thinking and action on the part of a glamourous CEO's first action - on the first day – on the first hour of taking over the charge?

- Was it a pre- planned ploy on the part of NK to send a clear message that he meant business without wasting time in routine introduction and other formalities?
- Was it a clear strategy to send message across that he would decide and dictate his terms as he had accepted the toughest mandate of influencing and changing the 102 years legacy of Durbs – the most challenging task?
- Was it a message that people including his senior leaders should expect him in doing things differently?
- Was it to impact the collective culture of the organization from the very first moment since we know that collective culture is an aggregate of what is common to all of its group and individual mind- sets. Perhaps the thought behind was that such unique action on his part would obviously influence changing the mind sets of hundreds or thousands of people?
- Was it that his thought process was driven by clear idea of doing things differently in his each steps of action?
- He might have thought that majority of the people being basically typical 'followers', should be influenced from the very beginning to think of change and for that it was important that they realise the new leader's style is not going to be stereo-typed.

Within the span of 15 years, 52 % of Fortune 500 companies and 51 % of FTSE (*)100 have disappeared from their respective lists. Inability to adopt to changing scenario was cited as one of the key reasons.

(The FTSE group – a UK listed blue chip company, designed to measure the performance of the 100 largest companies traded on the London stock exchange touched upon this figure).

Cultural Mosaic Leadership

NK swung in to action pretty fast. The leading global management consultant in head hunting of leadership level talents, already had facilitated the promoters in identifying and attracting some of the best-in-class senior leaders from the leading organization. Newly formed four new strategic business units saw the stepping in of four most successful senior leaders coming from best-in- class FMCG with classy background of IITs, IIMs or from similar top ranked premier institutes with successful track records. Almost all the critical support functions were taken over by the successful seasoned senior professional leaders who joined from organizations of repute. One of the key focus during attracting and selecting such stalwarts was beside those incumbent's competencies, the emphasis was on their possessing aspirations and skill to own up challenging responsibilities and drive change.

One of the most interesting point was that these successful leaders came from multicultural background. They came from a combination of reputed MNCs, classic leading Indian corporates and even two of them from overseas organizations of repute. Therefore, amusingly, they came from varied work environment, different set of values, culture and also were accustomed to certain behaviours while leading.

I guess that's what precisely underpinned NK's increasing importance of leadership in those day's complex business environment in Durbs. Beside managing the multicultural leadership team, the challenge was also to produce results.

So, NK had to deal with the interesting challenge of forming a winning team of leading through his skill on ' **cultural mosaic leadership** ' as the newly joined senior leaders came from a blend of ethnic groups, from different regions of the country including few of them from overseas too, and with different culture, possessing different DNAs, varied leadership styles and beliefs. And they stepped in quick succession too.

So, the promoters along with NK probably had strong strategic mind set of how best to deal with the new team of senior leaders coming from varied cultural background. NK clearly focussed on four major aspects while framing the canvas of strategic interventions.

Canvas of strategic interventions

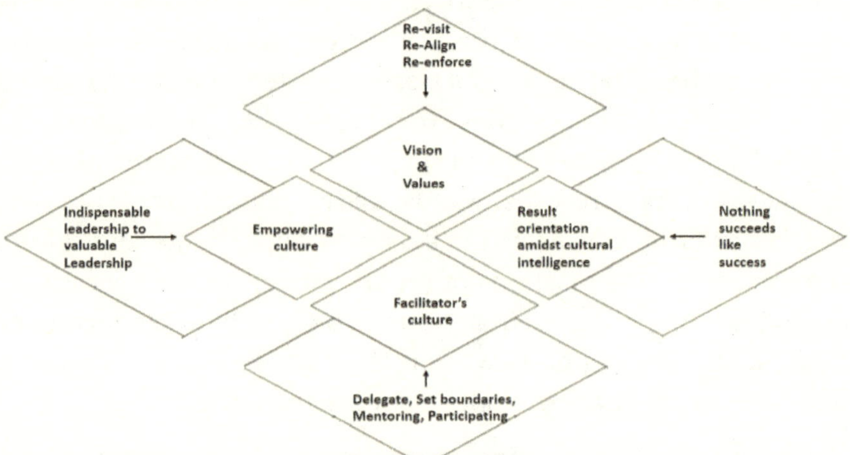

And the four key dimensions were as follows:

i. **Vision and values – alignment by breaking down cultural barriers –**

Leadership had the toughest cut out tasks of ensuring the vision and core values are re-created or rather co-created where participation of leadership team was ensured. It was important in view of the fact that many successful leaders who were attracted to join Durbs, came from varied work culture, values and accustomed to certain behaviours.

Conscious about the cultural mosaic leadership, NK therefore ensured that appropriate respect was given to new leader's view point while collectively focussing on re-creating the vision and core values.

ii. **Result orientation amidst cultural intelligence –**

While leaders from varied organization culture stepped in with their dream to contribute significantly, it was important for the Promoters, the Board and the CEO to tackle the challenge of aligning everyone as managing a multicultural leadership team is toughest though could be rewarding too. Working closely with leaders from diverse backgrounds and facilitating them to create a 'delivery orientation culture' was most interesting task.

NK had the toughest challenge of caring the views of such new leaders but somewhere he had to be 'polite but firm' in driving home the strong message that leaders had to be productive in delivering their challenging agreed goals in quickest possible time. Guiding principle was however, encouraging collaborative work while producing result.

iii. **Facilitator's culture –**

From a control freak culture of leading team, the top management was conscious in creating an environment of facilitator. It was basically moving away from boss culture to facilitator's culture.

iv. **Creating 'empowerment oriented culture'** but ensuring that such empowerment is given to the right leaders. The effectiveness would happen once not only the CEO but one or two level below the CEO also starts delegating such concept down the line. Its consciously shifting culture.

It was the promoters who first thought bringing changes and then the new CEO with his ideas of disrupt, destruct, construct, initiate change aligned the entire leadership team with such objectives.

Harvard Business School Professor John Kotter spoke about management is coping with complexity whilst leadership is about

coping with change. Leaders are responsible for setting direction and aligning people whilst managers manages budget, organize events and solve transactional problems.

Remember this:

Let's highlight a relevant and interesting subject of 'Cultural Intelligence (CQ) referred in an article from Centre for Creative Leadership (CCL ****) wherein they spoke about need of the top leaders to possess while leading multicultural team.

The article captured interesting views from Soon Ang (****) the author of several books on Cultural Intelligence (CQ). She felt cultural intelligence is a person's capability to function effectively in situations characterized by cultural differences. 'By culture', she notes that ' we do mean national culture but also other types of diversity like age, gender, ethnicity, profession, organization, religion, socio - economic status, sexual orientation, and others. People with higher cultural intelligence orientation, would be better decision maker in intercultural situations'.

Soon also clarified the difference between Cultural Intelligence and Emotional Intelligence. She said – 'both in fact include capabilities that facilitate effective interpersonal interactions. Emotional intelligence is critical for leadership effectiveness with focus on detecting and regulating emotions. Whereas cultural intelligence focuses more broadly on cognition, emotion, and intentions of self and others, and explicitly on intercultural interactions.

Though multicultural aspect touched upon here was more from global organization's perspectives having employees/leaders from different countries in one organization but the concept or the skill highlighted here would be of immense importance to the leaders in any Indian organization.

Accordingly, new terminology of "cultural mosaic leadership was coined from the perspective of explaining NK's leadership style as he could attract talents from different organizations both from India

and overseas and obviously those resources carried their respective perceived values.

And another smart strategy of 'building organization' was that after populating the senior leadership positions with high performing leaders, the focus went in next six months guiding the Human Resource team in putting in place a highly effective management trainee scheme.

The objective? The strategy?

Idea was to "catch them young and groom them up with your way of working" by attracting young potential top talents from best of the business and engineering campuses. Through this route of attracting talents, within four to five years, the organization reaped the benefit of availability of smart young home grown adequate bench strengths of talents who were available to gradually replace the average performers.

A cross function team consisting of senior leaders with right passion and aptitude with facilitation from the Human Resource team were given the responsibility to create a highly effective, relevant to the business scenario, a 'Management Trainee Scheme'. The scheme gradually became one of the best-in-class programme which in subsequent years created enough of interest in the premier campuses across the country during those years. Such initiative inter-alia helped Durbs in a span of few years to become one of the 'preferred company' to work with especially at the management school campuses and such steps kept on adding value to the brand image.

The cross function – cross location exposure during MT period, challenging live projects under the best of the mentors, quarterly evaluation along with specific guidance on the learning progress was the key highlights. Focus was to get more young stars from the top fifteen premier campus of the country for sales and marketing, supply chain, procurement, R&D and few other critical functions. This continued for few years continuously till the HR and the top leadership team felt the numbers taken was adequate. Such constant strategic interventions across organizations contributed to re-positioning of Durbs as a transformed brand.

And most interestingly, few of such well-groomed managers also responded to the ideas of getting in to reverse mentoring role. It was quite exciting for them. Few of the seniors were keen to have such 'reverse mentors' for their own interest. Yes – the concept was well structured and the HR it. It had tremendous response both within the organization as well as to the huge number of leading B Schools.

Isn't it interesting to imagine how the strategic canvas looked like? Top of the pyramid had a good numbers of highly effective inspired leaders who were raring to contribute to the agenda of co-built, re-vitalise and reposition brand Durbs. And the customers (stockists, distributors, retailers) facing team at the forefront had best of the home grown talents through the MT route in addition to specific hiring of talents that was made through lateral entries.

Interestingly, with such massive shake up in people strategy, the top management team could deliver the **'coup-de-grace'**. Simultaneously, within next six to eighteen months, a good number of non- contributors, average performers across all levels either left the organization or were weeded out!

OLD WAYS

WONT OPEN

NEW DOORS

Barring the well - orchestrated top management team in 'Durbs' who shouldered the responsibility of the transformation, the rest of the organization were obviously curious to know where they were heading and what the organization was trying to accomplish? The top team under NK realised that it would be unwise to assume that majority of the workforce instinctively would know what the collective goal was!!

Having realised the above, NK and his top leaders with the encouragement and participation of the promoters dived in to the significant task of addressing the vision and core values of the organization.

Much to the excitement, the leadership team picked up the idea of tackling the key issues through debate and transparent discussions. And the mandate was to have structured workshops to arrive at resolutions to the challenging and complex issues. The 'off-site' workshop concept gained high acceptability and venues around 'picturesque Rishikesh' in classy wellness retreat provoked the senior leaders to address not only the Vision and Core Values but it helped in addressing and prioritising other important issues. Most importantly the vibrancy and bonding amongst top 25 leaders were visible to the rest of the organization members – that's key to team work and team building.

The serenity of the location impacted. A top ranked organization development (OD) facilitator got involved in setting the deliverables of such 'off-site workshop' which prima facie focussed on co-creating the vision and the core values. And in the next 6 months, through 2-3 'off-site workshops' the team could finally develop the vision statement and the relevance of the Core Values in building business objectives. Simultaneously, they could develop organization building objectives too - thus it helped in articulating to the rest of the organization about the leadership team's aspirations, key goals and most importantly what was expected from the 'people' while accomplishing such tasks and how would it address the motivational level of people?

An innovative strategy to demonstrate to rest of the organization about the 'collaborative leadership' in driving down the significance of Vision and Core Values across organization was taken up as key task!!

Doing it differently?

Reinforce the importance of Vision and Core Values to keep pace with business growth plan.

- It was one of the chilled winter afternoons in the northern India part of the country!
- Venue - In the newly built large state of the art auditorium!
- Location – Delhi. At the new Corporate Head quarter's elegant glass house of Durbs!
- Year? Around 25 years back!
- Audience – A packed venue with presence of 175 key members including the zonal business heads of all the SBUs.

The auditorium was elegantly decorated with lights, flowers, diya. The fragrances of high quality insens impacted the mood and greeted the audience. Dais was thoughtfully done up with innovative digital signages which appeared to be ahead of time, innovative but attractive posters on Vision and Values were prominent. Entire setting ignited the audience who were curiously waiting for the unfolding of the events!! One could feel the divinity all around.

NK took the centre stage. Elegantly drove home the essence of the newly crafted vision. Articulated with simple but relevant examples of every words of the vision statement and its relevance. Communicated the task ahead for all the leaders assembled and did not leave the dais before getting commitment from members of the assembled large number of leadership team about their driving the agenda in their respective areas of operation.

Uniqueness of leading change through walk-the talk of collaborative leadership style continued much to the delight of the 175 key leaders. A well-orchestrated master plan in terms of owning the responsibility of driving the vision and the core values – the first of its kind in the 102 years company charmed every member.

Once the vision part was addressed, the audience were further charmed when they witnessed that the seven core values were explained by seven key senior leaders (mostly from business side) who came up to the dais one after another.

Commonality amongst the seven leaders while articulating the seven core values were:

i. simplicity of the contents,

ii. explaining relevance of each of the values in building organization,

iii. citing simple examples while explaining the context with reference to expected behaviour,

iv. most importantly the expected responsibility of the assembled leaders in owning up creating appropriate awareness on core values,

v. and ensuring the spirit and essence of the each values to be percolated down the hierarchy of each member across geographies.

The entire team much to audience's pleasant surprise could internalize few important decisions through announcement from the CEO, at the fag end. In essence, they were:

1. The CEO himself would own up initially as a one year project to ensure the success of driving the Vision and Core Values.

2. Each of the seven top leaders would champion or rather own up one of the values which they articulated in their presentation. In other word, the uniqueness of the strategy was that seven senior leaders would henceforth have such task incorporated in their KRA.

3. Similarly, in the first year the other key leaders across organization reporting to this seven top leaders would have henceforth four KRA in building businesses and one KRA in driving Core Values.

4. In every quarterly business review session, the progress of the task pertaining to driving Vision and Core Values had to be shared and would be evaluated too.

NK, the key change navigator perhaps felt that to stand out in driving the agenda, one has to do the things differently in all aspect of business without losing one's uniqueness while leading. Perhaps his leadership thought was influenced with the thought that try going with 'what you feel more than what you think'.

"The mediocre teacher tells. The good teacher explains. The superior teacher demonstrates. The great teacher inspires". -

– William Arthur Ward

In an organization where strategic initiative in people management had been lacking, where over a period of time the job security plagued the performance orientation culture and mediocrity were predominantly a trend, such interesting initiatives were well appreciated by majority of the workforce and subsequently realisation happened that it contributed to the growth strategy of the organization.

A very relevant quote from R E Disney – ***"It's not hard to make decisions once you know what your values are".***

Key idea

"Coherence among your strategic intent to change, your setting performance priorities and re-vitalising your culture would create high impact to both the employees and the customers too. Corporate history of transformation has proved time and again that employees and customers would be 'glued' to such initiatives".

Company culture is a natural by-product of people working together. Whatever be the culture of the organization, that culture can get influence with positive impact and can accordingly change as organization evolves. To build the desired culture you desire, prime importance would be to have the inspiring Vision and establishing Core Values. To establish the Core Values, its essential that leadership team need to keep them relevant as part of the ongoing conversation.

Views of Joe Reeves of ARGI (****) are interesting. His views were: "While building a company, usual focus of the CEO is on product or service, market, getting folks to help you to sell your product or

service. Rarely do the CEOs begin by thinking about articulating the vision, core values your future employees should have and that's where Joe felt that it could lead to fatal flaw for the business".

He emphasised on focussing on a few critical shifts in behaviour and justified through an interesting and relevant example on people's behaviour. He shared a study that only 10 % of people who have had heart bypass surgery or an angioplasty make major modifications to their diets and lifestyle afterward. We don't alter our behaviour even in the face of overwhelming evidence that we should change. Change is hard. So you need to choose your battles.

NK and the key leaders must have thought while taking over that creating the vision and core values inter- alia with the clear endorsement of the promoters would be the exceptionally powerful tasks in view of the prevalent scenario of the then Durbs. In addition, perhaps he had the advantage of getting 'insight views' of prevalent culture vis a vis the culture needed to transform the organization from none other than the promoters.

NK and his key leadership team therefore, might have felt strongly that the exercise of developing Vision and Core values would enable Durbs to codify it's organization Vision, Culture by purposefully distinguishing the elements that are unique, strong and positive.

He might have sensed that as Durbs grew over a period of last few decades, it might have outgrew the values that were thought of at its initial stages. Perhaps he was confident right from beginning of taking over that Vision and Core Values were not set in stone. A company is a living breathing entity that changes over time. Change is constant and a universal truth! With the constant change, the work culture would get positive impact as one make new hires, re- position the brand, reorganise the organogram with altered deliverables.

There is no way around it – change is corner stone of business. As the company evolves, so should its Values. But the challenge is that rarely the CEOs begin by thinking about the vision and the core values that their future employees should have. It could lead to disastrous results. This pattern of thinking is not only seen in Indian companies but there are so many articles from overseas authors that this challenge is there in overseas organizations too. Human Resource team can take the lead to ignite the leadership to own up such tasks. But perceived challenge is that HR at times also under transactional work pressure, loses focus on such interesting aspect of their role.

(Interestingly, in the next chapter, we dealt with an unique case. Its different. It's about the newly joined CEO's while taking over a complex and challenging task, had some other strategy in mind. With clear homework and study of the situations, he decided to address from the first day, first hour tackling the fiery issues of revenue first since it was a question of survival. CEO after addressing the initial fire by 'walking the talk' first tried stabilizing the revenue flow and then subsequently took up the Vision and Core Values.)

Katherine Hutchins (****) a talent acquisition professional in one of her write up cited an interesting data on the above. A 2005 survey of large employers (overseas companies) reflected that 90% had a core values statement. But there had been a doubt about the employees internalizing such vision and core values. Thirteen years later, an unscientific poll covering almost 100 HR professionals, revealed that majority of them had clear doubts that most of their employees would not be able to recite their company's core values.

Assumption could lead us to believe that almost similar scenario would prevail in the organizations of our country too though silver line on the bleak is that many progressive organizations are getting into innovative and structured approach in developing Vision and Core values meaningful to their employees. In view of constant changes in dynamics in businesses, many of them are revisiting the defined Core Values and the organizations are not hesitating to alter it but, yes of course, with participation from all corners.

Developing the Vision and Core values is not only a complex and challenging task but it demands commitment and the efforts from the top management. It might be a toughest task but the reward would be phenomenal. Surely this would make the organization purpose-led and in turn would drive home the competitive advantage.

While the above chapter projected the strategy of 'change navigation' initiatives highlighting significant role of the promoters and NK - the first change agent, Durbs continued its glorious journey of constantly repositioning the organization ahead of time. The leadership team, post NK's departure after his close to four years of association, continued their significant contributions. Subsequently, we saw them achieve the distinction of getting in to the status of being in the top ten 'Best Place to Work with' amongst Indian corporates. Durbs with their excellent leadership today has turned out to be a global entity with the availability of their classic products across more than 100 countries!! Significantly, their plant units are present in almost 10 units outside the country. They have already captured a market share of approximately 28 % which is phenomenal achievement and they would surge ahead further. Interestingly, in pursuit of spreading their wings globally, almost 31 % of their international operations are contributing to Durbs overall sales revenue. Shareholders value enhancement has been admired. And let's hope such glorious journey would continue. Doesn't it sounds like: "owners pride – neighbours envy"!!

The strategy of NK in driving change management and his success reminds us of a citation from an interesting episode where describing the factors of one of the CEOs success in change management, she felt that what changed her was the message of freedom that she obtained from her investors and the board. She also felt necessity of the freedom to feel one's own fire, to lock inside one's self and make one thoughts edible. Interesting indeed.

"Transformation is a journey and not a destination".

3

INDISPENSABLE LEADERSHIP VS VALUABLE LEADERSHIP

Embracing the future is the key trait for reformative leaders. This chapter is about a true story of reformative leadership. While many organizations spend time on succession planning, but this story from a global giant MNC goes much above the essence of typical succession planning. A philosophy of building organisational leadership that had been institutionalized.

The touch points of this story is also about setting aside one's own need in favour of serving others. Does it sound similar to Maslow's theory of beyond self – actualisation? Yes, indeed.

"Fostering leadership culture of reformation".

- **Leading beyond succession planning – story from a glamourous MNC story.**
- **Driving culture from Indispensable leadership to Valuable leadership – episode from a large Indian MNC**

Let's share the classic story from a leading MNC and my learning from that top ranked global MNC, a pharmaceuticals and health care giant on strategy to their unique succession planning and their strategies on valuable leader versus indispensable leader.

Jodhpur – Rajasthan, the vibrant destination of desert, palaces and kathputlis. A wintry evening in an imposing palace, basically an ancient huge fort which once upon a time use to belong to famous kings from the bygone era. Now renovated and converted in to a heritage - super classic star hotel. We, a team of 35 HR professionals of the company along with four top management leaders from corporate just sailed through two and half days workshop with pre-structured agenda on people strategy in this classy royal venue.

Structurally, the third day of this glamourous MNC giant post afternoon used to be 'relaxed informal open house session' with the top bosses. Such session was followed by the grand cocktail dinner. HR leaders of the plants, regional headquarters and corporate office were keenly waiting for this session as specially they wanted to interact with their recently announced boss – the President HR, Mr Roshan Bharucha.

Let's look at the role of this four top leaders who had spent quality time through frequent interactions with us throughout the workshops. Just before they came to Jodhpur, the organization had announced the strategic rotation of role at the key leadership level which was part of usual organizational development process and it's also in line with such key leaders' career progression perspectives.

i. Bharucha had been in the organization for two plus decades including a two years stint in a neighbouring country as part of his career development plan which incidentally used to be anchored by the global HR head quarter team in UK. But before this, in the last three years he was the President of Finance & Accounts.

ii. The last three year's President HR - Mr Anal Patkar moved to take over the Finance and Accounts in place of Bharucha.

iii. The other two eminent Presidents who were present in the workshops all throughout was the President – Marketing and Sales and the President – Units and operations.

iv. Mr Vishal Kanwar, the President Marketing and Sales who also had fairly long stint in the organization had no change in his role/assignment.

v. President – Units and Operations earlier had a stint of two years in two key areas namely Quality Assurance and Commercials.

In the informal interaction session at the fag end of the workshop, the four key leaders basically were encouraging participants to raise their points, doubts or pick up any organizational issues which were always of paramount interest to the top management. After few initial queries from my colleagues, followed by answers from the four bosses I raised the key points which led to interesting interaction mode.

Q from me – 'We see rotation in the role of key leaders like you periodically. Interesting no doubt - but what could be the key philosophy of the top management behind such rotation of role and responsibility at that level'?

A (RB - the new HR boss) - "Listen, such steps are part of the HR global policy. The strategic HR from Global Headquarters in consultation with key global leaders keep on developing their HR practises. Once they are ready with any new or altered version of any people related policy or practises, they obviously would share their plan with the MDs of the various countries where volumes and values of businesses would be quite high and the MDs of such countries in turn would keep their channel of communication down the line on such developments".

Patkar (AP) who was basically a specialist in people management, picked up the thread where RB had finished his view point. AP shared the objective rather rational of such move in clearer terms since he was not only holding the President - Human Resources but was in touch with the Global HR Headquarters in view of his role and position.

AP – "listen, the strategic HR team at the UK Headquarters follows certain processes. They have their communication channel regularly with the MDs and Head of Human resources across the globe. They usually would keep few important points in mind while rotating or changing the role of the MD minus one level leaders and prima facie the points would be:

i. Performance and potential of each such leaders which includes a comprehensive assessment processes.

ii. Such senior's aspiration on his/her career advancement

iii. Individual's preference in moving in to generalist's role where in future they could be the country head and not necessarily in his/her own country but could be in other country too. Or whether such individual leader would prefer to remain in their specialist's role only.

iv. All such important inputs help the strategic team to have clear developmental goal of the key leaders.

Me – interesting and thanks a ton!

VK, considered as one of the most successful leader chipped in. He added interesting dimensions since he had gained knowledge about the philosophy of people perspectives of UK leadership team in view of his frequent participation in important strategic issues in various global forums.

VK – See beside all those important points, let me add that Head Quarter strategic HR team would also involve the selectively potential leader so identified to be associated with 'lead cross function projects' where one can have members from neighbouring countries too. Obviously, such chosen leaders while contributing to the specific project would have to stretch him/herself a lot as their main KRA remains unaltered. Objective perhaps could be to see performance under stretched target, initiative, passion, collaborative leadership skill, ability to handle cultural intelligence while interacting with project members from other countries etc.

Such strategies of rotating the key leaders surely must have helped this MNC giant to develop their top talent pool in multiple functions.

I had picked up one of the very interesting learning when AP shared a philosophy of the top management:

AP – Look dear friends: one of the strategy of such move could also be that we as leaders need to be valuable rather than indispensable in the organization. Let's elaborate a bit:

It's better to be valuable leaders rather than becoming Indispensable leaders -

Anal Patkar who had led the people perspective successfully for a good amount of time in this organization elaborated the concept much to our delight. The essence of his views were:

AP – "Indispensable leaders" are important as they must have attained that status in view of their sheer dedication, hard work and business contributions. So, let's recognise their calibre. Such leaders usually tend to become 'workaholic' type. Over a period of time, they tend to be irreplaceable. Such indispensable leaders are usually strong in delivering the results. They would build team but experience reveals that In view of their personality type, attributes, they are emotionally attached to their role. They don't bother about the working hours or work- life balance when it comes to job issues - therefore, at some point of time such a trend could lead to burnt out which becomes not only a common phenomenon but ultimately the organization suffers. I guess all of you would be conscious in not encouraging such situations.

Therefore, the strategy of creating a culture of developing valuable leaders through such periodical 'role rotation' is being encouraged by the strategic global HR team of our organization.

"Valuable leaders" – So, our sort of MNC is clear on leadership strategy that encourage the culture to develop mind set of becoming valuable leader instead of being indispensable leader. For HR & their learning and development team the strategic agenda need to be adopted that how collectively we create a culture where leaders firstly internalize the concept and then can be supported to get developed on both mindset and skill set of how to be valuable to our organization. Being valuable, essentially would indicate that one need to be always curious – raise key points on important business discussions. Challenge the status quo and encourage team members to think differently. Valuable leader need to be engaged and obviously would be a smart contributor beside the aptitude of hard working. A valuable leader should be conscious to understand where to draw a line in terms of his/ her getting in to operational or transactional issues while dealing with their team – rather at some point of time s/he need to stay away and encourage team to drive things. In other words, such leaders need to develop the skill of self-regulating their tasks and pressure of work. They should be skilful enough to balance relationship with their task, relationship even at personal level with their colleagues and be conscious about how to stay healthy and ultimately should enjoy happiness.

Another critical attributes the organization would like to see in each of the valuable leaders, is 'humility'. They must at each stage be open to new learning. Over confidence on learning would invite fall of the citadel. **"True humility is staying teachable regardless of how much you already know".**

You all are playing pivotal role in managing people dynamics across geographies of this great organization that collectively all of us have built in. This session must have provided you with the opportunity to pick up the thread of learning from this well thought 'periodical role rotation' and the fundamentals of 'creating valuable leaders' specially at the senior level. We are confident that you all would keep such ideas while developing your people strategy when you guys go back to your respective locations".

What a lovely session it was – It ignited our thought process. Raised the collective spirit of ours. Charged us enough to rush quickly to get soaked in the other spirit – the spirit of single malt at the cocktail-dinner venue which was ready to greet us!!

While Anal Patkar's focus was emphasising on creation of culture of having valuable leaders rather than indispensable leaders, few of us subsequently took this topic up in our professional forum to seek some more experts view. Some interesting dimensions emerged on the indispensable versus valuable leadership:

- One clear view emerged that in an MNC sort of established organization, presumably the systems, processes, policies are laid down clearly. Effective leadership is important but system would ensure that at each level there would always be enough of bench strength of talents which in other words ensures a structured approach in succession planning too. Therefore, culturally indispensability is overshadowed by valuable leadership.

- The other view was interesting too. It highlighted the pluses of having indispensable leadership. According to **Ken Sundheim (****)**, the CEO of a New York based executive search firm, Indispensable leaders are capable of driving revenue, maintain sense of optimism around the team members, accepts full responsibility for the performance of the team. They understand that each day of leading is a challenge and embrace the hurdles they encounter rather than avoiding or ignoring obstacles. Ken felt that such leaders mostly would be unwilling to accept defeat as their traits would focus on alternatives in the event of hurdles which would ultimately lead to uncanny monetary improvements. Interesting indeed!

- Let's acknowledged the view of **Ronesh Puri (****)**, the MD of a leading executive search firm in India. Incidentally he is well known to me and had partnered us in some business assignments in the past. According to Ronesh, the traits of some of the successful leaders, many a times have paved the way to the upsurge the rise of indispensable leadership in many of the leading promoter driven or in other word, the family – owned businesses. Times of India in one of their news publication also had covered Ronesh's views in defining those key traits of such leaders. He was specific in sharing his interesting analysis based on his vast experience in dealing with the Corporates:

    i. Owners are passionate and emotional too about their businesses. Therefore, the intelligent leader with their humility, high EQ, would understand these aspects of the owner and would adapt to their working style. Leaders with high ego generally would end up in unpleasant confrontation.

ii. Family owned business at times are unstructured. Hence, such successful indispensable leaders usually possess the skill of producing results amidst ambiguity.

iii. Usually traits of such leaders would make them successful in the area of good people management skill – a trait which any family owned business entrepreneur would prefer.

iv. Usually the owners are very hard working. Hence, they enjoy the company of leaders who can possesses the ability to work hard and sincerely while producing results.

v. Most of the promoters or owners of family–owned businesses are well exposed to 'hands on' approach. Hence, they expect their key leaders who can roll up their sleeves and sort out issues at the ground zero level.

vi. Finally, the successful leaders tending to become indispensable too, should have ability to respect the values of the company which is usually being spelt out by the owners. Once the successful leaders passes through the ' tested and trusted ' concept in the eyes of the owners, they tend to become indispensable and they adapt to other important aspects like appreciating the organization's eco system which is simple, informal, straightforward, unstructured with high result – and bottom line orientation, Risk taking ability is encouraged and therefore, financial rewards are also lucrative. Decision making is pretty fast and reward mechanism is also very fast.

On a fine morning, one could realises that leaders demonstrating such traits and skills consistently, have already won over the trust of the promoter. Such leaders therefore would also be perceived by stakeholders to be in the horizon of being indispensable leader.

An interesting observation of an young 'People Manager also appeared to be logical. She felt that a leader who attained the level of 'indispensable leader' in her/his organization, can also be seen or perceived by employees as truly valuable leader! Well, interesting indeed and organizations would be delighted to have such kind of leaders to lead!

Wrapping up

Varied views are always a healthy phenomenon specially on such interesting topics like this. Hence, perspectives shared by:

- Anal Patkar focussing more on valuable leadership
- Ken Sundheim' view on indispensable leadership and
- Ronesh Puri's analogy of leadership traits in promoter driven or rather family – owned businesses are interesting.

Debate on such views are not the objective here. Various factors may influence style of leadership. Philosophy of the Promoters, strategic direction of the Board of Directors in inculcating specific leadership style to achieve complex business objectives, Business model, Strategy to steer revenue, Core Values of the organization, also leads to emergence of specific style of leadership.

But having gone through all such views, **Ken Sundheim's** (****) view on methodology of measuring how indispensable you are, was no doubt interesting. He felt that answers emerging out of the four key questions would make it easier for organization to adopt specific style on whether to have a culture of having more of valuable leaders vis a vis indispensable leaders?

Many a times we all have come across circumstances that individuals while expressing desire to resign from the job in anticipation that s/he being one of the most indispensable leader would certainly be retained by authority with higher compensation, or promotion should first measure how much critical s/he are to the company's success.

To measure the degree of your being indispensable or critical, answers to those few questions perhaps would help you to evaluate or assess the situations:

- Situation 1 – Are employees or clients likely to leave if you depart?
- Situation 2 – How much disorganization would result from your leaving the Company?

- Situation 3 – How much would morale of the colleagues suffer due to your departing?
- Situation 4 – Would the revenue be badly impacted on your leaving?
- Situation 5 – How long would it take to get the replacement for you?

Well, the answers would make it so easy to measure degree of one's indispensability. Similarly, answers to such situations would also help the management to decide whether to retain such critical resources or not?

Beside the above, such views that would come out from the questions would lead the top management to introspect and decide what sort of culture they would like to encourage in the organization? Should one focus on encouraging culture of having indispensable leader(s) or the strategy should be to focus on building organizations where there would be adequate bench strength of potential performers in critical roles so that organization does not suffer when indispensable leader (s) decides to quit?

The organization has to ponder on probable answers of all those five questions and then re-assess or review the leadership scenario. While discussing such hypothetical situations with my few senior colleagues, I enjoyed their view points when they brought some interesting dimensions while responding to each of these five points and those are:

- Situation 1 – where with the leaving of a leader, why his/ her followers also would also decide to leave the organization?
- If we have created right leadership culture, than a true leader would ensure that business continues with contribution from each members even after his or her leaving.
- Situation 2 – Why would there be disorganization consequent to the leader's leaving the company? Valuable leader would surely ensure process and systems were in place and under no circumstances there would be disorganization on any member of leadership team's leaving.

- ☞ Situation 3 – Yes! Initially the employees might feel low or disheartened to see their leader leaving. But a true leader would have nurtured the culture of "organization is larger than individual".
- ☞ Situation 4 – Why would there be apprehension on challenges in getting replacement of the leader? A true leader must have ensured enough of talents from within who could be the right successor consequent upon the leaders leaving the organization.
- ☞ Situation 5 – Leader's key role is to groom his/ her identified deputies who could be his/her successor. So, in the unfortunate event of the leader's leaving the organization, the organization would not suffer.

We experienced a unique case of a top leader's leaving the organization and it was in a promoter driven organization. This leader, had a wonderful track record of contributing more than a decade in not only to the healthy bottom line but also helped the Brand to grow. He took all sort of measure in ensuring that he attracts a right candidate as his replacement through a process and finally the recommended incumbent was inducted. The Board and the Promoters had enough of confidence in agreeing to the selection of the candidate. Their comfort perhaps was more on trust of the senior leader's respect and commitment for the organization. That's the kind of image he could built over a period of time. And interestingly, the new leader in shortest period of time justified his induction much to the comforts of all stakeholders.

In a personal chat after few days of our classic leader's leaving the organization, my curious mind raised the point of his being proactive while taking care of recommending replacement and that too a very good resource. It was wonderful learning. Let's share what all he had to say:

a. "I have contributed in co-creating the brand. Helped the organization to be reckoned as a leader in the Industry.

b. My own market value, image in the Industry went up high in view of our establishing this organization as one of the best-in-class organization in the Industry.

c. I have enjoyed thoroughly in building up this business brick by brick during the last decade and half.

d. Rather the excitement had gone deep in my vein and being one of the co-architect, I played role of an entrepreneur and enjoyed the challenging journey through out the period I was in this organization.

Therefore, even if I decided to leave the organization, would I not agree to the point that it becomes my morale obligation and responsibility too to see the flag of the organization remains high in the market place? Hence, I also have important role to play in contributing getting the right replacement. If such commitment doesn't come from my 'thought process' then isn't it that my conscience will haunt me?

Focus point:

Such mentality, such classic moral intuition, such devotion at work can only be from the classic leaders who moves beyond the theoretical definition of leadership. Was it that closer to Maslow's higher motivational theory of 'beyond self -actualisation'? Such extra -ordinary leaders would like to see that their contributions are well remembered by people even after they leave the organization or even after they disappear from this planet. That's the psychology perhaps influences them to grow and shift their focus towards grander goals and aspirations.

Shannon Mcintyre (****) in the column of greater good magazine during February 2007, shared that Maslow subsequently named such motivational level above self – actualization by terming it as "self – transcendence". At such level, the individual's own needs are put aside, to a great extent in favour of service to others. The theory also highlights that purpose of life is not to perfect oneself, but to transcend oneself by connecting with others. This is radical new understanding of one of the dominant theories in modern psychology.

4

THE TRIED AND TESTED WAYS OF STRATEGIC HIRING

Great talent is scarce. And the scarcer the top talent becomes, the more companies that aren't on their game will find their best people cherry–picked by competition. Amidst such dichotomy, the CEO would continue to be responsible for managing profit.

Well, this chapter dealt with our unique learning experiences on possible hurdles of getting talents who could be smarter than their superiors. A survey through analytics on such subject highlighted the following points:

i. high performing leadership teams are 400 % more productive than average ones. And the gap rises with job's complexity.

ii. Failure to attract top talents was the number one issue in the conference Board's 2016 survey of global CEOs - before economic growth and competitive intensity. Alarming – isn't it?

iii. a whopping 82 % companies don't believe that they recruit highly talented people.

iv. Alarmingly 87 % of the experts dealing with talent acquisition believes that their current acquisition strategies was not going to work.

And with such discouraging scenario, how can one expect transformations?

One of the most important initiatives should be to how the strategy to attain success in attracting smarter guys. Talents we identify must be brighter than us. But hurdles are galore. Let's know the honest answers to such fundamental question from the bosses – the interviewers – the assessors – the selectors that how many of them would really be comfortable with such objective of attracting talents smarter than the reporting mangers of the candidates sitting on selection panel? Well, your guess possibly is right!

The chapter also dealt with sharing of experiences including certain relevant behavioural science aspects.

Won't it be interesting?

- **Transformation would remain as myth unless leaders create culture of attracting talent smarter than them.**
- **Experience sharing from a promoter driven large organization**

Mckinsey's Steven Hankin (****) coined the term

"war for talent". Even after twenty five year of introduction of such expressions, the war is still on or rather going to intensify.

Ideally, successful leaders would strive in attracting and hiring C – suites executives who could bring skills that successful leaders might be lacking. If you have smarter guys than you then you don't have to baby feed them. If you hire people who have lesser skill and knowledge than you, you would be building pocket - sized company. The reverse is that if you hire guys smarter than you than you are going to build one of the most admired company.

Easier said than done!

Successful entrepreneur philosophy that we have witnessed over a period of time has been that "I am not the smartest leader in my company. If I possess such mentality, my company will never grow".

It sounds so simple an idea but reality is something else. Get in to 'self'-talk' mode and seek the answers while making unbiased self - assessment that:

i. how many of us during most important task of leadership level hiring, have consciously recruited incumbents who were more superior, more smarter than us in all respect?

ii. How many leaders while selecting their subordinates were comfortable in recommending or selecting candidate whose compensation was higher than him/her?

We all have come across such situations in our journey of talent acquisitions. And we can guess the answers!

Most of the corporate leaders possesses the tendency to be indispensable. Nothing wrong in it! Indispensable leaders brings to the table certain unmatched traits. But if we try and be surrounded by smarter colleagues having higher level of knowledge and perhaps skills too that would in turn upgrade our own intelligence.

Let's share a relevant interesting views on transition tenets from **Jeffrey Hollender (****)**. He was the executive chairman of Seventh Generation (SG) company dealing with household and personal – care – products. His views also encompasses the importance of attracting talents smarter than the bosses.

Jeffrey after growing the organization to a height started realising about hurdles in achieving further ambitious growth. His inner alarm was triggered by two key points. 1) success of SG could be vulnerable to other threats 2) while deciding to take on greater role, he needs smarter guy than him who can supplement his improvement areas. The key step he took was objectively assessing his ability to lead SG to an ambitious growth. In that process, he discovered his limitations. His bold self - evaluation made him discoverer that his limitations bled the benefits of his staying on as CEO. It's the courage of giving up your coveted seat and that too on a juncture when you are growing your company reasonably well. But of course when your inner wisdom says that you can add more value by moving in to more challenging role and let the new leader navigate the company to newer heights. How many of us would dare to think in such strategic direction?

Well, coming back to the chapter, let us glance through on the key topics of attracting smarter talents than the bosses.

I was enjoying a rap session with a small group comprising two seasoned Human Resource professional, two of my key business leaders who were well known for their talent assessment skills and two senior talent acquisition professionals who had been associated with the leading brand of 'HR search' firms. The common views emerged that few leaders often tends to have psychological threats or hurdle in selecting talents who might outclass them at subsequent stages at the work place which might in turn dent their 'indispensability'.

While collective views were interesting to know but let me share the view of Sohal which was relevant to this chapter. With rich experience of two decades, Sohal was well known in his domain of 'search' assignments for the leadership level hiring. He was from a leading brand of HR consulting firm. He highlighted his experience on this point. Here is the gist of our conversations:

Sohal – "I was invited to be part of the selection panel of a leading FMCG organization where we were responsible to partner them in their search of key talents. It was during the interview of a candidate for an important leadership level role. One of the interviewer initiated discussions sharing a complex business case. Then he invited the candidate to respond. Incidentally, the interviewer was the reporting manager of the position for which we were interviewing the candidate. By the way, he had a long and successful tenure in that organization climbing up the ladder from the middle management level. He was perceived as a leader who could deliver business results but was also known for his 'authoritarian leadership' style too at times. During the mid of the conversation, he took a pause. His face sounded more reflective. Then he briefed the interviewee of a tricky problem highlighting a business case. To me, it appeared almost like an 'in–basket exercise' to assess the candidate's skill though the problem shared was fairly complex and bit difficult for candidate at that level of hierarchy. He then invited the candidate possible solutions on that complex case study. It was clear from the body language of the interviewer that he was deriving joy with the assumption that the candidate would surely fumble in sharing the right solutions to the case law and perhaps in the process the interviewer would try to establish his superiority in terms of knowledge or skill than the candidate.

MSD – "Sohal, interesting indeed. Yes - we too experienced such mentality of few assessors. Let's acknowledge that many of us gets trapped on such syndrome that you just highlighted.

Rajesh Iyer, one of senior business head of a leading IT/technology company who happens to be my friend too, having rich experience of working in leadership role with couple of leading companies stepped in with his views.

RI – friends, unfortunately, not many organizations have laid down processes on review mechanism about style and effectiveness of interviewers while hiring talents for CXO level! I wish the HR leaders of organizations lays down structured training programme on interviewing skill specially for the leadership level role.

Usually, the seniors while interviewing don't have the ideas or feel it necessary of seeking feedback about their interviewing skills. But relevant feedback would always be well accepted by leaders who believes in self-development too. But such feedback has to be highly qualitative and effective. Perhaps such practise of feedback if institutionalised would serve two key aspects:

i. Overconfident interviewers would have opportunity to convert those feedback from experts to their personal developmental plan.

ii. Once interviewers conducts the process with elegance focusing on key objectives of assessment, then the interviewee would enjoy the interaction irrespective of outcome of interview results. This in turn would contribute to the 'brand building' of the organisation.

We all know that interviewing rather interaction in the era of 'war for attracting brightest talents' specially at the leadership level is all about

MSD – friends, during my tenure of working with a top Global MNC, I had most interesting learning. I experienced my Director HR, the well - known persona in the industry, use to step out of his cabin to walk down to the reception area every time when he had to interview a senior level candidate who use to come and report to the receptionist. Mind you that during those days such level of director use to have their highly effective personal secretary to facilitate such task to their bosses. But I never saw him using his secretary on such occasions. The Director HR, on reaching reception area one floor down would always first introduce himself. Than would greet the candidate. And finally use to invite him/her to his cabin exchanging pleasantries while walking back to his cabin.

- Isn't it a demonstration of height of humility?
- Isn't it smartly show casing bit of organisation culture?
- Won't such gesture bring immediately high level of comforts to the candidates?
- Won't it contributes towards building the brand for 'most preferred employers'?
- Our ego – centric mind, our mindset on possessing the superiority complex in view of the position that we hold, being obsessed with the glamour of our position, our hierarchical driven mentality are few of the hurdles that if addressed appropriately then we can create the right ambience towards our efforts of making organization a best place to work with.
- Would the organization culture be an issue to be looked in to?
- Or is it that right training on interviewing skills can address such mentality?
- Or is it that handling elegantly interview process is 'leadership style' specific?
- Or is it that successful leaders are born with the superb skill of working without ego?

- Or is it that as you grow up in the hierarchy, your wisdom helps you to do things differently?
- Or is that nurturing by our 'role models' or mentors who are excellent assessors could make huge impact?

Friends - being a seasoned player in the area of talent scouting and assessing, let's listen to Bhawna Jain on her perspectives on such interesting dimensions we collectively touched upon.

BJ - A classy leader in the HR domain with a professional background of social science brought interesting dimensions. She is a classy player in behavioural science area and has been quite successful in her close to one and half decades of experience in best -in - class companies.

Bhawna said – "Look, my little bit of knowledge on such area, prompts me to touch upon few points:

a. possibly a sense of 'insecurity feelings' prevails amongst few of us while attracting smarter talents for the team.

b. It could be due to lack of self–confidence.

c. It could also be due to apprehension of losing our so long 'authoritarian leadership'.

d. Our superiority complex at times influences us during interviews. The undesirable belief that we are far better, affects us. With such 'self – feelings' we develop exaggerated opinions of ourselves".

With a smiling face, Bhawna paused a little and continued saying:

"let me not get in to academic mode on the topics of behavioural science as plenty of such views are available even from the eminent specialists or even in the google. But I was impacted on the views of famous **Alfred Adler** (*****), a prominent psychologist dealt with concept of inferiority complex long back. He touched upon this topic. He felt that superiority complex peeps to human mind due to a reaction to a deep feeling of inferiority. Well, this was interesting to me and I had gone through enough of these theories though this could be a debatable point. But if we are conscious about such views of experts then it would help us to deal with situations more consciously and effectively".

We complimented Bhawna for bringing such 'insights' specially her sharing Alfred Adler- the eminent psychologist's views. Indrajeet Gupta, a successful CEO of an e- commerce organization who was keenly observing and listening to such conversations while complimenting every one for sharing their views started giving his view point.

IG – Specific instances of interviewers behaviour at times had baffled me that how come being seasoned interviewers for leadership hiring they at times demonstrate may be unknowingly, immature way of conducting themselves during interview. Bhawna touched upon the causes and effects aptly. Yes - our ego at times unknowingly pushes us to ignore the ideas of others. I am aware of a leading coach who shared that while spending quality time with his mentee, they together use to discuss the effects of ego and how to deal with. He use to facilitate his mentees through role play, examples etc in driving home the key points of differences between confidence and arrogance, humility and weakness. These are important learning I had.

Well, so far collectively we discussed various points about our ego, superiority complex, feelings of indispensability, lack of humility while assessing etc of few recruiters which blurs their foresightedness on the benefit of recruiting smarter guys than them. Having said that, I also feel that such leaders could be easily identified and then facilitated by specific coaches or senior HR leaders possessing effective mentoring skills. Let's acknowledge that such shortcomings can be addressed easily. Let's accept that after all, such senior leaders are successful professionals who reached to senior level by virtue of their significant business contributions. Such facilitations would bring more wisdom to them and make them evolved leaders".

MSD – "I tend to agree with you – IG. Well, my experience on such subject in MNC, leading Indian corporates and promoter driven organization reveals that results are much better in organizations where the 'hiring processes' including the assessment process is well laid down. But effectiveness would go up further if we can also introduce the process of periodical review on effectiveness of interview skills, structured feedback mechanism. Members of the top management team – specially senior level Human Resources leaders ideally should own up such process.

Successful organizations, mostly articulates the career path especially at the senior level. Top management makes it sure that leaders can inter–alia earn more feather in their coveted cap once they master the art of taking courageous decisions of recruiting smarter resources than them.

Once Organizations enjoys the benefit of having such mature leaders, the organization would reach to newer heights".

Sohal stepped in and felt: "look, many of the C - suites level recruiters including senior leaders of Human Resource's talent acquisition experts believes that they possess all the tricks in terms of assessment but interestingly lets accept the fact that as a human we can be blind to our blind spots too. So, lets remove such undesirable belief. Better idea would be to invite specific domain experts from outside the organizations from time to time who could be even mentors. They would be able to add value in assessing critical areas of knowledge and skill where we might not be that strong.

Such strategies and interventions would surely take the organization to newer heights. And therefore, lets me conclude with the powerful quote from **Mark Twain (****)** –

> ***"When you hire people***
>
> ***that are smarter than you are,***
>
> ***You prove-***
>
> ***You are smarter than they are'.***
>
> ***- Mark Twain***

Let's remember this:

It's interesting to glance through the views of Kara Goldin, (****) the American business lady, the founder and former CEO of Hint Water. She viewed that whenever someone seeks her advice on hiring, she would quote Steve Jobs (****) as she derived highest inspiration on Steve's superb advise that:

"It doesn't make sense to hire smart people and tell them what to do. We hire smart people so that they can tell us what to do ". Kara felt that in her long journey of years in interviewing and hiring, she realised that most of the candidates makes effort to show case how genius are they possessing all the answers. That never impressed Kara. Instead, she believed that effective leaders are not looking to hire a smart, competitive, know-it all who constantly would try to outshine every one.

Kara felt that one key reason of her being successful was that she always tried to be humble about what she didn't know and therefore, tried to be surrounded with people who are more knowledgeable than her. She felt working with people who don't think the way she thinks, is much better as it helps to get varied opinions which helped her and her company to grow.

Her views became an interesting headline:

"I would never hire the smartest person in the room". But why? She went with her opinion that smartest person in the room would lack interest in spending time around people who are more intelligent than them. So, it won't help to make them (or their team) better at their jobs. By not being smartest person in the room is not about the dumbest person in the room. Instead, it is about not believing that you are the smartest person in the room".

Difficult? Yes. But make sense? Yes.

Isn't it interesting? Isn't it mind boggling?

5

THE TWO SIDES OF A COIN – "LEADERSHIP DECISION VS TERMINATION AND GRIEF HANDLING"

Common phenomenon amongst successful leader's beliefs is that their talent, capability are significantly higher than the people they are leading. Why not? Isn't it preferable? Yes, of course unless it's perceived by the followers as superiority complex of their leader.

Well, officially there is no reports on mental health diagnosis on superiority complex. Leaders with unrealistic sense of self – esteem might develop superiority complex about their abilities. Such leaders tend to make quick judgements on various aspects including their people and there could unintentional biases too on such leaders' part!

Amos Tversky and Daniel Kanheman (****) believed that such leaders might also develop syndrome of having cognitive biases. It enables such leaders' brain to prioritize and process large amounts of information quickly leading to mental short cuts. While the mechanism could be effective, but it's limitations can cause error in thought. Point of concern! Isn't it?

Therefore, this chapter focusses on an actual story emphasizing the importance of leading dispassionately even if the leader has to be task oriented from the revenue point of view.

- **The story on Pride of the corporate architects for standing up their values while terminating an employee at leadership role**

  vis a vis

- **Who measures the depth of the grief - Other side of the coin?**

The other day, I was in a monthly review meeting of one of the most promising SBUs where I am an advisor too. The monthly business review was being anchored by the Siddharth Mehra, the CEO of that business. My interest inter–alia was more on how Siddharth, the CEO who joined probably six months back was going to deal with the business review mechanism. My watchful eyes could figure out in no time that Ramesh was not in the review meet and it was surprising to me as being an young talent in the arena of business development role how could he be missing the business review meeting. I just whispered to the ears of Siddharth that why was Ramesh missing? and Siddharth buzzed back that once the meeting was over he would talk about it.

Meeting got over and Siddharth and I moved to his cabin.

Siddharth – "Ahhh Ramesh'.

"Siddharth took a pause and then in a polite but firm voice said" We have asked Ramesh to put down his paper and leave'.

MSD – "Well, Well ...I interrupted".

"Ramesh is only few months in your system! I recall you and your HR were quite upbeat in your communications that how important it was to attract such key talent like Ramesh to strengthen the list of C – level executives. Hearing you, we were fascinated with the prospect that his knowledge and skill on bringing digital intervention and technological innovation would increase the horizon of business in newer areas too".

Siddharth – "Yes, let's acknowledge that he possesses those qualities and in fact, he shared some brilliant business ideas too. Siddharth continued:

Siddharth – "He could have been a stellar performer in the organization. But unfortunately we had to take a tough stand of getting rid of him as in-spite of repeated counselling by my HR, he could not bring improvement in his interpersonal relationship. He lacked the temperament of being a good team player and most importantly tried to push his ideas only. Views, suggestions or ideas of his team members were never given an iota of importance leading to demotivation in the team. He appeared to have possessed the leadership style of "my way or high way "while dealing with his team members. I kept on wondering on possible reasons of such behaviour. Certainly these attributes are contrary to our Core Values. Even my effort to counsel him did not produce any result. Well, you know – the organization had to move fast amidst tough competition and we had to take a decision pretty fast – that's it".

Key Points emerging from CEO, Siddharth's assessment:

Was it that Ramesh's nurturing happened under an autocratic leader?

Or was it that such traits of commanding mode he got developed during his grooming in earlier days?

Or was it due to his natural response in his mind to a sense of losing control over the points that use to draw debate from other team members?

Or was it that such debates or countering his view points by other members during business meeting or specific situations developed stress or fear in his mind of losing grip over his thought process while interacting with others?

Or was it a case of his possessing inadequate trust factor on others? The neuroscience experts said that trust is an important component of human social life. But trust deficit refers to the lack of belief or faith that one could have on his superior officer, team members. This may happen due to lack of belief factor. Couple of reasons could be there such as egocentric behaviour, lack of empathy from seniors, communication gap between leader and his team members.

Sidharth continued – "look, such behaviours are contrary to our Core Values. Incidentally, my strong counselling also did not bring any impact and hence the unfortunate decision of asking him to leave had to be taken".

A conflicting feelings rather mixed emotions influenced my thought process. One aspect stood out clearly where I complimented Siddharth, the CEO for taking quick and firm action. I could clearly sense from the body language of my CEO which was essentially – Pride. Pride of the CEO for standing up their Core Values by taking a tough call!!

But who measures the depth of the grief?

– Other side of the coin!

But equally interesting was the other aspect - my emotions - as I was still struggling with the dilemma that was it a right decision on the part of Siddharth the CEO in getting rid of Ramesh in such a short period? In fact, magnetism of my 'people oriented mind' was provoking me to seek opportunity to meet Ramesh, a promising leader. Thoughts after thoughts were splashing down my mind:

i. Was it that our mind works like a speculative machine and therefore, it produces unlimited or rather infinite stream of thoughts?

ii. Were we justified in terming him as an autocratic leader in such a short time? Isn't it that at times our task orientation drives us to be tough?

iii. Was it that our selection process was not appropriate?

iv. We had multiple round of interviews to ensure we select the right incumbent in the key leadership role! Was it not therefore, we collectively failed in our assessment of Ramesh? We were known as a progressive organization. Our HR processes were perceived to be effective. I) we had good practises of forming selection panel with specialists having wisdom in assessment, ii) discreet reference check, iii) application of psychometric tests, iv) in basket- exercise during assessment, v) confidential reports and recommendations from the leading HR consultant who identified Ramesh - so on and so forth.

Even then why still there would be doubts on our assessment skill of candidate and that too at the leadership level? Why would there be unpleasant instances of asking a senior leader to leave the organization apparently unfairly and it happened with in few months of Ramesh's joining when doubts were raised on his leadership skill?

Few more aspects flashed in my mind about Ramesh's case. Those were:

i. Was it that Ramesh was not oriented effectively by CEO and HR where usually a new leader gets fair perspective of culture, core values which includes importance of showing respect for the people?

ii. Was it that he was not counselled, coached adequately when leadership team started observing issues in his leadership style?

iii. Was it that the CEO, the HR Head was not empathetic while listening to his point of views too?

Well, my mind was still keen to listen to what all Ramesh might have been going through with the tough decision of getting removed so quickly after his accepting the new job.

Another story - Qualified professional with two decades of corporate experience had to quit his job in view of growing unpleasantness –

Vishal after spending three years in an important role at the corporate function started facing unpleasant pressure for the last few months from his superiors. Tough behaviour, mounting demand in performing tasks even beyond his area of work, compelled him to stay back late hours almost regularly. Such situations started affecting his personal life and his family of wife and son also started getting jittery.

When it reached to the stage of unbearable for Vishal any more, he had no choice but to leave the job even before getting another job opportunity as he felt that being a qualified professional in an important corporate function grabbing a job should not be that difficult.

Poor luck – even after nine months of best efforts, Vishal could not grab an offer! This includes his failed attempt through appeal to his CEO to get back the job. Even his idea of appeal to the Chairman of the company who was also known to be fair employer having empathetic views toward his people, went in vain.

Financial challenges, challenges of handling mounting expenses including the most important one of son's education, dealing with pseudo – empathy, difficulties in dealing with irreverent questions of neighbours, relative, friends forced him and his wife to reach to highest level of frustration including loosing self – confidence.

Desperation compelled Vishal along with his wife to reach to the Chairman's office. With folded hands, both of them bowed down to touch the feet of the Chairman when tears were dropping down the cheeks of Vishal. His wife apparently could control her emotion and she focussed on appeal to get any sort of job. The embarrassment of the Chairman could be clearly seen. He then gradually started giving both of them comforts and talked about interesting philosophical points and even cited inspiring examples from our mythology.

Well, the HR was advised by the Chairman in Vishal and his wife's presence to discuss the issue with the Chairman and both finally left the office. But let's try to co-relate the issue with view point from **E Stanley's victorious living (****).** Going by theory of E Stanley, such steps on the part of Vishal's action might carry a sense of incompleteness and frustration, but not of guilt. Victorious living does not mean perfect living in the sense of living without flaw, but it does mean adequate living, and that can be consistent with many mistakes".

Let's ponder on what provoked the family to take the difficult decision of visiting the office of the Chairman to put up appeal? Such steps are usually unheard of. One should try and understand mind of the couple and not the action they took.

Was it mere frustration which is basically more of a negative emotion? Frustration crops up sensing feelings of uncertainty and insecurity. Such feelings stems from the sense of inability to fulfil needs. Blockage of such needs will bring more of uneasiness and more frustration.

Idea was to internalize the pain of vishal and his wife as to what they went through. There could be hundreds of similar painstaking episodes around the corporate world. Performance deficiencies need not to be accepted – true. But should not there be better ways of dealing issues of separation or termination? And we pondered on such issues hereafter.

"Consult not your fears but your hopes and your dreams. Think not about your frustrations, but about your unfulfilled potential. Concern yourself not with what you tried and failed in, but with what it is still possible for you to do" –

Pope John XXIII

Termination can be life –altering for the person being sacked, their family members and even their colleagues. We know that it can also impact the spirit or morale of the team members or even can be an unnecessary gossip point in the corporate corridors. One would wonder what all the family members in such cases might have gone through in dealing with the sudden and unexpected decision of cessation of service. Lot of questions and thoughts hovered around my curious mind. Children of today's generations are smart enough to speculate that there must be something unusual actions happening around their 'papa's or mom's' job. How does this impact the kids mind would be interesting to know though in professional world, the professionals manages to get the next job sooner but at times it might take longer time as it's not easy to grab the right job in a competitive world. Besides, how would one deal with the curious neighbours who are smarter in realizing that their next door neighbour might have lost his /her job.

'Masala for gossip' in our society. How one would handle such unfortunate possible social stigma?

Therefore, all these could also lead to stigma associated with mental illness. We may relate such situations with Goffman's (****) basic definition. He identified the main elements of stigma such as labelling, stereotyping, social isolation, prejudice, rejection, ignorance, status loss, low self - esteem, low self – efficacy, marginalization and discrimination. It leads to emotional issues and suddenly such issues becomes strange things to deal with!

For the workman category however, at least the Government machineries have introduced long back the "do's and dont's" while taking decisions on dismissal or termination of workmen. Compensation also has been mentioned in labour laws though such benefits mentioned in the acts also needs reviewed in view of the changing landscape of Socio – Economic and Industrial Relations scenario. Therefore, views are being expressed that provisions of social security acts needs upward revision specially when termination happens in a short notice.

We are yet to be strong like some of the country of the western world in terms of offering adequate social security measures or contractual clauses in the employment agreement safeguarding financial aspects of 'sudden firing'.

Severance packages in our country are far from being adequate. Well, at the senior level the trend of negotiating adequate severance package as part of the termination clause is becoming a trend. But it has so far been unstructured and what happens to the plight of employees who are at middle and junior level?

Let's ponder that isn't it that time is emerging where the business leaders of the several professional forums of the country, the senior leaders dealing with people, various employers forums, the trade union leaders, every banners of the leading political outfits, need to spend quality time on this sensitive subject of adequate remedies?

The moot question becomes a professional being hired after following proper processes of selection including best possible assessment tests during multiple rounds of interviews. Even the collective wisdom of selection panel members clears the final selection only when they get satisfied with various assessment reports/comments of interviewers and finally their own judgement after getting satisfied with the incumbent's being strong enough in his/her aptitude and attitude during interviews with them.

Therefore, sudden decision of the reporting manager endorsed by his/her superior manager asking an employee to leave with in few months of his/her joining and that too in a responsible position could tarnish the brand and corporate identity beside inviting other unpleasant issues..

Should we not therefore, see reasons to the fundamental views that:

- Was it a wrong selection and if be so, should we not review the role and effectiveness of interviewers?
- Should there not be review on fairness of the decision of termination? Well, organizations might have laid down processes on such sensitive issues but reality remains that voice of the concern employee's would always be suppressed with various pleas which could be created by reporting manager.
- Therefore, fingers usually are always raised on the employee stamping him/her as incompetent. Would it be wise for the Corporations to ideate role of an independent seasoned professional whose role or assignment may be that of a Chief of Ethics or Chief of Corporate Values, or Chief mentor kind of.
- Such professional need to be highly mature, be positioned at higher level, should be reporting to Board and ideally should have well accepted image. While there has to be structured process about their role but fundamentally such role inter – alia would be to facilitate leaders to internalize the essence of Core Values. She/He be able to eradicate any sort of biasedness in our behaviour and decision making. In addition, right counselling, coaching, mentoring of leaders around would gradually pave the way of building 'trust' of people in organization's decision.

One of the idea could be to pick up potential business managers who are already in 'fast track' career path. Put them for six months or a year under such chief of ethics officer. Let them ideate and contribute to such subject. But clear communication is key that such ideas or steps would instil more wisdom in the individual to lead. Such role is to nurture them towards higher role. Let them come back to business thereafter. The result would be phenomenon.

The issue remains with creditability of our decision making process, ethical leadership practises, adherence to Core Values, fundamentals of 'walk – the talk'.

In addition to the Corporate endeavours in nurturing and developing the fundamentals of ethical leadership, it would be wise idea to introduce elementary lessons of such subjects right from the early stages at the Educational Institutions. And fortunately there are encouraging initiatives happening around to propagate such initiatives.

It's heartening to talk about an unique initiative by a leadership institute. The Peter F. Drucker Foundation for non- profit Management. It's in New York but has its presence in other cities of USA. The institute is known as **'Frances Hesselbein (****)** Leadership Institute'. In line with their goal and mission it is providing social sectors leaders with essential leadership wisdom, inspiration and resources to lead innovation to vibrant social sector organisations. Isn't it so encouraging? While developing next Gen leaders, they are going to focus on developing leaders of Character and competence and also would provide dynamic global mentorship".

In our country, **Ramakrishna Mission of Delhi (****) – ref TOI)** also has ventured in to innovative reforms in the education system. They have created an unique programme called 'Awakened Citizen Programme' for their students which is a three year course containing 16 interactive modules are aimed at bringing out student's infinite knowledge, power and goodness.

In the recent time, we came across news coverage which highlighted **IIT – Indore's** (****) introducing an unique course teaching ancient classical scientific texts or rather Indian science in Sanskrit starting with 'bhaskaracharya's mathematical treatise 'lilavati' of almost a thousand years ago.

There must be many more of such sort of initiatives and what great ideas are all these. Let's imagine the impact that we might witness if we have thousands of such initiatives from Government level, Industry bodies, Private Sectors, Management and Engineering institutions. We would then reach to a newer horizon of workplace where amidst drive for revenue, the happiness will be the key 'Mantra'. Even I am tempted to think of having capsule modules of such programme which could be initiated by each and every schools of our country". Once such ideas are propagated from the early life, it would have higher impact.

Such focus on initiatives centred around Ethics and Value base leadership's humble presence would take the humanity to newer heights amidst change of reins to next Gen leadership. Outcome of such collective ventures would enable us to visualise the sense of purpose in the arena of education including management education and leadership development where key focus would be on developing ethical or principal – centred leadership. People across hierarchy would obviously be at the centre stage of any such initiatives ".

6

THE POWER PARADOX: "ETHICAL LEADERSHIP PRECEDES BUSINESS SUSTAINABILITY"

Leaders attains heights by virtue of their attaining skills. Such exceptional leader's ethical leadership traits separate them from the pack. It fetches trust, respect popularity, power and silent support from followers. Interestingly, such skills would deteriorate unless the leaders are conscious about corruptive influences of power.

This chapter through a story from a corporate world, dealt with the power paradox. It's about importance of how leaders can consciously stay away from the corruptive influences of power. Else, beside losing the position, the followers silently would withdraw their support leading us to poverty, be it moral or ethical!

- **Ethical leadership precedes business sustainability -**
- **The Power paradox -**

Down to penury lane -

Morale...Ethical...Organisational

"A LEADERSHIP STRATEGY WITHOUT ETHICAL CLARITY PRODUCES MORAL AND ETHICAL BANKRUPTCY "

- BILL DONAHUE

The business landscape has witnessed sensational changes over last few decades as we witnessed significant rise and falls of some established brands. Experts reasoned through their analysis the cause and effect of such rise or fall.

Having deliberated on ethical and value based leadership, let's through an interesting story, touch upon one of the causes of 'collective failure of leadership' and relate it with dichotomy while enjoying power.

The Management Gurus while attributing reasons at macro level for fall of a Brand/Business might have felt i) complacency of the leadership team, ii) inability of the leaders to adapt to technological changes, iii) lack of foresight of leaders, iv) strategic misjudgements of the top management v) poor execution ability vi) repositioning or nurturing the Brand amidst competition, complexities in the market and many more.

We would deal with an interesting story of one of the successful and fastest growing organization. But unfortunately, after few decades, to utter surprise of all corners, one fine morning people witnessed the unfortunate fate of its suddenly knuckling under and was about to shrink like the gigantic ship - Titanic.

Well, there could be many prime reasons of such sudden descend in the business results, but we kept the focus of discussions here from the leadership styles, traits and effectiveness perspectives only. The story has been formatted in few steps to represent it appropriately.

Stage 1

"Srimart" the company, within two and half decades of its stepping in to Industry, created niches in the market presence. It moved ahead of competition and was enjoying huge market share. Srimart was considered to be 'owners pride – leaders envy' sort of organization! Being a listed entity in the stock market, the share price soared. Joint ventures with glamorous global brand further consolidated the Return on Capital employed (ROCE). Keen interest of Private Equity players and their participation in the investments further augmented the financial growth. AUM value (asset under management) ascended steadily. Organization could attract bright talents across levels and focussed on best people practises. Shortly the company started getting reckoned in the market place as a 'preferred organization to work for'.

Stage 2

A passionate leadership team surged ahead overcoming every hurdles be it within the organization or in the market place. The DNA or rather the success mantra of leadership team was being coined as 'entrepreneurship, innovation and passion'. With such traits being demonstrated by the management team, it was obvious that more authority, more empowerment, delegation of power would be extended much to the satisfaction of the key leaders.

Perceived views of many other members was that with such recognition, 'feelings of pride' was bringing also a sense of confidence amongst the majority of the leadership team. Interestingly, few of the other senior members had different views as they worked closely with the key leaders. They felt it was rather overconfidence and not confidence that was growing.

Stage 3

Well, did all those success factors also contributed to being overconfidence? So was it that excessive belief in their abilities made them to overlook the fact that they might go wrong too? Was it that such overconfidence started bringing an element of underestimating others?

Was it that key leadership team started believing about their being unparalleled and therefore they possesses uniqueness in their dealing with any challenges?

Well, such traits could be good to have but certainly carries certain percentage of risks too.

We may encourage ourselves to boost our self – esteem – not bad! But once it crosses a permissible limit, it would bring in arrogance. Belief of the experts are that overconfidence also creates judgemental error as it leads individual to overestimate their own accuracy. It also makes individual more dominating and for them it is hard to accept that they could go wrong too.

It reminds me of the quote:

"there is a thin line between confidence and arrogance.....It's called humility. Confidence smiles – arrogance smirks".

Humility is the key word. Management Gurus for decades have rated this trait of humility as one of the key factor to be successful leaders.

In Srimart's case, the quality might have dipped a bit amongst some key leaders when success galore was kissing them. It happens but this is where real leaders makes the differences.

Stage 4

Overconfidence were also perceived as one of the tough hurdle in reaching to the company's goal. Experts believes that with such trait one is likely to be overly optimistic about his/her abilities and prospects. Therefore, we start believing that our decisions are best. Was it that such avoidable perspectives led gradually to wrong decisions?

In addition, instances of biasedness during decision making process was observed to be widening. Strong liking and disliking cropped up - and it was not only while dealing with team members but disastrously it was happening also while dealing with vendor partners, selection of customers, even while taking measures during collection or recovery of hefty dues.

Rampant failures in keeping commitment in various aspects were also being cited as collective failure of leadership team. Respect which the leaders earned over a period of time, started descending. Perhaps complacency contributed to the leaders not realizing the fact that they had earned respect from the people for their leadership qualities. Was it ignorance or overconfidence that they failed to realise that erosion in leadership qualities would obviously lead to withdrawal of respect by their people. It is one of the fundamental points of failure of leaders and in turn organization's failure. Being a significant point, let's discuss it afterwards.

Views of people on few of the leader's suddenly being extravagant in leading their life style and possessing suddenly disproportionate assets became unnecessarily corridor gossip points. Abrasiveness in their behaviour might have also contributed to the deterioration in relationship.

Leaders who initially emphasised on zero tolerance on integrity, respect for people, were being doubted about their ability to 'walk- the talk' and deviating from such Values. Lack of alignment of purpose and actions with Core Values were distinctly visible.

The 'Nasha'- the Euphoria, of becoming more powerful – omnipotent, getting second wind by all means, the growing glamour and its challenges, over confidence, hungry for rewards, immune to risk, complacency, bit of arrogance and many more of such traits might have dented the foundation of 'principle - centred leadership ' which in turn hollowed the spirit of Core Values.

'Power begets power' sort of environment was conspicuous by its presence and it was not conducive to congenial atmosphere. Was it that all these were indications of risking of setting flame to the towering inferno?

Simultaneously, the growing unfavourable business results, falling of share prices amidst losing of confidence of the share - holders, seeds of discontentment from within and also from outside the organizations including various governance forums, the growing differences in strategizing while driving business between key leaders and the stake holders, uncertainty in growth of business and therefore, loosing of many potential performers across levels, all put together started denting the image of the organization.

Many members perceived the erosion of humility – the greatest asset of a successful leader, was one of the key reason of its people started disliking the leadership style. There are umpteen numbers of instances where humility has been termed to be the key success of successful leaders. The more such leaders climb up the ladder, the more humbleness gets blend in their leadership style. Alas, as success was kissing the constant success of few of the key leaders, unfortunately their humility was evaporating. Added to it was unpleasantness created often with the abrasiveness of some key leaders. What could be the destiny of a company in such situations?

Yes – you could guess it rightly!

And stage 5 – consequences were inevitable?

Yes indeed! Writing on the wall was clear! Well, there could be umpteen numbers of reasons to the downfall of the business but we kept our discussions here on the lacklustre leadership which unfortunately had to witness the erosion and fall of the citadel.

Remember this:

"The causes are the effects of prior causes". The idea of inevitability arises from the thinking of cause and effect. Nothing happens without a cause. If we say that causes produces certain effect, we mean that it's inevitably followed by the effect, as long as nothing interferes with the process. Well, these are established theories.

'Causes and effect' leading to such disastrous situations could have been louder discussion points but instead, the views of specialist in the paragraph below be viewed on such issues.

Behavioural scientists opined that human mind has tendency to reject the idea that everything which happens is predetermined and inevitable. To many intelligent people, this idea at first sight obviously is perceived as inconsistent with experience and common

sense. But if we think a bit logically than we will realize that this inevitability arises from the logic of cause and effect. Interestingly, the causes are the effects of prior causes'.

Other views differing the above came forward that many events in our daily life is accidental. Sounds logical? Yes indeed!

Let me touch upon a relevant point to tune in on the stage 5 point which says, 'consequences were inevitable'. **Barry Simon's (****)** 'simple approach to philosophical questions' is interesting in relation with my points on leadership behaviour attributing to erosion of trust of people on them. Let's look at Key idea given below:

Key idea:

Barry opined that At any given moment we are usually motivated by many different forces. And when these motives conflict, the strongest combination of forces wins. And causes us to act accordingly. Perhaps physical desires dominate, perhaps emotional needs, perhaps duty or pity or love. What determines which one? Of course the combination of motives that wins is simply the strongest. Its strongest before we act. We inevitably behave in accordance with the causes i.e. the motivational forces existing outside us or inside us, at that moment. The complex pattern of external and internal motivation does simply only one possible response. Our conviction that at any given moment several alternative actions are all real possibilities is mistaken".

Was it that at the later part of fast growth of business, behavioural pattern of few senior leaders got altered. Certain undesirable element while leading business were observed by their followers which they felt were grossly counterproductive. Well, these are debatable points.

Dichotomy of power – The power paradox

Our knowledge, skill, attitude coupled with our emotional intelligence, potential, learning aptitude, respect for people, integrity, empathy, growing humbleness, etc leads us to success in our workplace. Such traits, fetches more trust and confidence on the leaders. It comes from all corners of the hierarchy and makes the leaders gradually more popular in the corporate corridors.

But then in many cases comes the urge of kissing quicker success, to grow up the ladder on a fast – track, taste more recognition, more fame, more financial benefits. Stronger influence of 'power begat power' and expectations of more authority starts peering the mind. Those who are keen observer of leadership behaviour must have noticed that while sailing in to the glamour of success, empowerment, popularity, fame some of the successful leaders develops the feelings of indispensability which cripples their mind. Such unsought traits also affects the leaders unfortunately who so long could stay away from influence of pride or arrogance.

Added to such erratic behaviour, many of such leaders at this stage perhaps tends to underestimate the importance of common man – the people, who only had given recognition and respect to those leaders. This could be disastrous.

But let's acknowledge that people could be smarter too then their leaders think. Once they observe erosion in the value system of their leaders, they would have the least of the botheration while silently withdrawing their support, respect any more to such leaders.

Focus point:

Such points reminds citation from one of the article of Henry David Thoreau (****). His view of a hundred seventy years still seems so apt here. He cited that "silence remains, inescapably a form of speech. I wish to hear the silence of the night, for the silence is something positive and to be heard".... "There are many things which we cannot say if we have to shout". He wrote as he contemplated how silence ennobles speech.

In the century and a half since, we have created a culture that equates loudness with leadership, abrasiveness with authority. We mistake shouting for powerful speech much as we mistake force for power itself. And yet the real measure of power is more in the realm of Thoreau's 'fine things'. Interesting indeed!

Alas! Corporates perhaps had always inadequacy of having capable mentors who could have mentored those erratic leaders applying Thoreau's theory!

We highlighted earlier the height of success to 'power – the failed leadership'. Let's get in to a fascinating points from Dacher Keltner (****), the author of ' The Power Paradox '. Keltner, is a professor of psychology at the University of California. Let's now corelate how we gain and lose influence from his write up.

Keltner shared a very interesting discovery during his research. He said – "While people usually gain power through traits and actions that advance the interest of others, such as empathy, collaborations, openness, fairness, and sharing; when they start to feel powerful or enjoy a position of privilege, those qualities begin to fade. The powerful guys are more likely than other people to engage in rude, selfish, and unethical behaviour.

Keltner termed this phenomenon as 'The Power Paradox'. People rise on the basis of their good qualities, but their behaviour grows increasingly worse as they move up the ladder".

(Don't we recall the commonality of such causes we witnessed in our career when we also observed the leadership behaviour specially where positive traits started declining amongst some of the key stalwarts who grew up the ladder? Significantly, it was one of the reason of downfall of 'Srimart').

I am provoked to share interesting analogy when Keltner cited outcome of another studies which showed that wealth and credentials can have a similar effect in terms of behaviour. He found that drivers with the least expensive vehicles always ceded the right-of-way to pedestrians in a cross walk, whereas people driving

luxury cars yielded only 54 % of the time; nearly half the time they ignored the pedestrian and the law.

Keltner has elaborated many more examples of abuses of power by powerful leaders. Studies show that people in positions of corporate power are three times as likely as those at the lower rungs of the ladder to interrupt co- workers, multitasking during meetings, raise their voices and say insulting things at the office. And people who've just moved to senior roles are particularly vulnerable to losing their virtues, his research and other studies indicate.

Keltner spoke about one of the recent poll of 800 managers and employees in 17 Industries. About half the respondents who reported being treated rudely at work place said they deliberately decreased their effort or lowered the quality of their work in response.

The abuses of power ultimately tarnishes the reputations of executives, undermining their opportunities for influence. It also creates stress and anxiety among their colleagues, diminishing rigor and creativity in the group and dragging down team members' engagement and performance.

The debate might crop up that why at an appropriate time effective counselling or feedback was not given to such leaders either by their superiors or Human Resource champions? It was fact that these leaders rose to such positions in view of their capability of producing best results through hard and smart work. They could have been facilitated to alter their undesired style of leadership and perfect themselves back to their desired stage of leadership. Well, learning point indeed.

Unless the top management and the senior leaders of Human Resources team focus on bringing effectiveness of the process of performance management – performance feedback, such change in behaviour of leaders can't be tracked and tackled. Fallacy in most of the corporate corridors about performance evaluation is that 'giving feedback' is the prerogative of the bosses only to his/her team members. Who would dare to care in giving feedback to powerful bosses? However, successful organizations would deal such issues with 'care and share' philosophy.

Silver line on the bleak was to learn that even during the period of impasse, the professionals, employees in general, business partners were confident that Srimart would bounce back. They felt that the legacy it has created, the infrastructure it has created, the large customer – vendor base it has created, the large investors that it has attracted, there was no reason as to why it won't bounce back? It was good to hear such positive emotions, confidence and trust on the brand even when it was passing through a dark tunnel.

An interesting idea from learning perspectives was floating around. We thought why not get in touch with few of the key senior leaders who might have left Srimart during last 4-5 years and understand their perspectives on possible factors that they felt could have contributed to the deterioration of Srimart. They might not have been there during 'downfall' period but might have sensed the fall of citadel well in advance and hence would it not be great to hear such views? In all, we could interact with more than 20 people. These 20 people were from CEO level, business heads, investment management function, risk and credit function and senior HR resources.

Specific questions were raised with them – of course individually with assurance that we won't divulge their name.

Questions we asked:

"Friend - Let's assume that Srimart has resolved all the burning issues. Poised to get back to its lost pride. And the Company offers you the role of CEO to navigate the journey afresh and bring the brand image, businesses back to its track. And you are fully empowered by the Board to steer the company. Based on your learning during your earlier stint, what are the few things you would do differently to lead?

Consolidation of the answers from those key leaders are penned down here but randomly. They were:

- Stay true to your purpose and align team accordingly (75 % of the respondents touched upon this point).
- Financial discipline (100 % respondents touched upon this point).
- Higher order stakeholder engagement (65% respondents touched upon).
- Focus on leveraging core opportunity to drive essentially your strategy/business plan. You need to identify a moat (60 % of respondents touched upon).
- Strong leadership team and they need to be in sync with core purpose. Essential to have ability to attract and retain talents (60 % of respondents touched upon).
- Core Values that the team need to follow has to be demonstrated from the top. Leaders essentially to develop the virtues of "walk the talk" (100% respondents touched upon).
- Ability to take medium to long terms strategic calls and have short terms goals that align with long term plan. This would then lead to decisions impacting allocation of capital, risk policy, resources etc (70% of respondents touched upon).
- Zero tolerance in dealing with Integrity (100 % of respondents touched upon).
- Last but not the least - Completely separate the three important bucket of ownership, governance and execution (85% of respondents touched upon).

Organizations would keep on facing challenges-success and failure. Challenges or failure has to be seen as opportunity provided we have the mentality to acknowledge mistakes. Perceived views reflect that there could be umpteen number of reasons for the downfall of Srimart. But the focus here from learning point of view was leadership aspects that might which perhaps could have also contributed to such downfall. We picked up the common points that people spoke about on such failures due to leadership issues. And deviation from Core values while leading turned out also to be significant. Our understanding and learning from Srimart episode was that unless leadership team is driven by their virtues, the Core Values would remain as theory and would only glorify the posters framed in the corporate corridors.

Experts feels that often we create confusion treating values and virtues as same – synonym. But there could be small but interesting difference between this two. Well, it could be a debatable point. Values are more of aspirations or in other word, what we intend to achieve or expect our people to achieve. While Virtues could be our possessing moral excellence through our behaviour.

Let's have an example to illustrate. Honesty could be defined as one of the Core Values. Its aspirational expectations. More of a theory. It projects our intentions. But it may not be achieved unless we demonstrate consistently our morale characteristic in remaining in conformity with such aspirational expectations through our beliefs and actions. Perhaps it's more intrinsic to one's DNA. Its remains deep in one's vein. It should be easily visible to others.

Somewhere down the line, was it that amidst defined Values, the moral excellence (our virtues) amongst leadership team was descending? Well, being a debatable point, what if you were to handle such issues with your wisdom?

Well, there would be umpteen number of business issues where the organization faltered. The purpose over here was to deal mainly with people and leadership perspectives.

7

"A PICTURE IS 100 TIMES BETTER THAN THE WORDS".

85% of companies have undertaken transformation initiatives during last decade and nearly 75% of those transformations failed to improve the business performance!

And this is from a report of leading international brand - BCG! By virtue of my three decades of leadership level role in three companies, I was fortunate to have worked with many of the leading global consulting brands who were reckoned for their strategic facilitation in transforming business. Yes – my experience is similar. Barring one story of success, rest all others that I had witnessed failed to produce the desire results.

What it reflects? The top management had always high interest in transformation as core objective. They had spent huge money, massive energy, enormous time, stupendous patience as their keenness was primarily reaping the benefit of transformations and taking their organization to the next level. But alas! The data of not only from BCG findings but my own personal experience reveals that mostly it was 'failed initiatives'.

The commonly used terms during such kick–off meetings at the board room use to be 'innovation', 'out of box thinking', so on and so forth '. But, let's for a second assume that the human minds – rather the company's leadership minds initially usually would lie low. Apprehension prevails. Those minds perhaps lacks clarity on such initiatives. In most of the cases igniting such minds had not been taken care of! Clarity on benefits of such projects for the individuals and the organizations are not clarified and hence alignment with the transformation objectives doesn't happen. Then how would such minds contribute to innovation, out of box thinking?

Learning from experiences of such high numbers of failed transformation initiatives, led me to the metaphor that transformation of mind should precede before any transformation initiatives. Else ....

I could relate similarity of my experience with that of **Tony Schwartz's (****)** impressive classic view. Well, usually the transformation assignments are centred around business model, structural elements, policies, processes, technology, marketing strategies.

May I classify Tony's key points briefly blending with my learning experiences too?

1. Organizations typically overlook the internal shift – what people think and feel – which has to occur in order to bring the strategy to life. This is where resistance tends to arise. The mind might get resistance cognitively in the form of individual's strong beliefs, deeply held assumptions and from emotional aspect it could be influenced with fear, insecurity. Addressing carefully such sensitive issues would be of paramount importance.

   Strategic intent of such transformation initiatives are to be clarified which includes obviously their faster growth too once such initiatives are successful.

2. Genetically and instinctively we put our own safety first, avoid taking risk and avoid unknowingly using our capacity for critical thinking to assess new possibilities.

3. While invitation to any company's leaders to be a part of any such important project carries importance to them but many of them might be carrying bit of inhibitions in their mind. Their position, authority, dominance, success gained over a period of time might have induced bit of overconfidence too. So, the top management's invitation to external classy brand of super

strategists, the management consultants, to drive important transformation projects might bring invisible 'heart burns' to the company leaders who so far were driving businesses.

4. Keeping in mind BCG data, Tony's view and my experience on reasons of many of such failed projects, I would tend to recommend that:

   ☞ much before the kick - off of such project of transformation initiative, invite a seasoned external facilitator who would be a specialist in behavioural science – also be a good mentor with knowledge of OD initiatives.

   ☞ Task? To address the mindset of the key leaders and bringing out comforts from each of them in order to align them to organization's objectives of such initiatives.

   ☞ Provide such expert with adequate briefing of the key senior leaders that organization would like to include in change management initiatives along with external strategic consultant. During briefing, provide SWOT analysis of the individuals and collective leadership team.

   ☞ Assign such specialist clear time bound responsibility on what to achieve.

   ☞ Beside effective counselling of the key leaders, both individually and collectively, take them to 'off sites' if need be. Skilfully facilitate such senior leaders on how to be move away from their comfort zone? Help them to be free from holding on to their mindset, ego, if any.

   ☞ Another key focus, The facilitator must encourage during such 'off – sites' the culture of creating 'open conversations'.

5. Therefore, transforming first the mind of the leadership team is pre–requisite. Wherever this aspect had been taken care of, the success would have kissed their doors. Two eminent psychologists **Lisa Lahey and Robert Kegan(****)** have termed this aspect as 'immunity to change'.

Yes- initially there would be cost angel too in involving such behavioural specialist, couple of 'off- sites', management time. But this would be negligible and to be perceived as 'wise investments'. If we have analytical data on cost perspectives of any 'failed projects', that could raise our eyebrows! Strategic intents are the driving agenda of transformational initiatives. If such projects are to be effective then imperative would be to first address such issues of people and their mind set which would also stimulate the positive culture.

8

CONCLUSION? NOT REALLY!

Let's begin a new beginning.....

"My paintings should become objects into which one could float, as in water, so that one's mind is hung...suspended, and the emanation of the painting would penetrate into people's consciousness"

– Douglas Portway.

We began our story with the first chapter's impassioned demonstration of the trade union members inside the super five- star hotel. And it touched upon relevance of Core Values during complex business issues. Since then we walked a long way mostly through story – telling mode on coherence among Strategic intent, Culture, Core Values, Business complexities and it's correlation with Leadership dynamics.

Interestingly, products are innovated constantly. Customers behaviours are dramatically transforming. Digital era has already revolutionised the Human – machine collaboration. High tech world has already been facilitating leaders to embrace collaborative intelligence leading to unlock increased productivity. This would in turn facilitate the emerging leaders to save huge management time enabling them to focus on higher- end transformational work. Corporate world is already witnessing the leadership journey's revolutionary shift. Interesting views and opinions are being floated on more dynamics to be witnessed on future of leadership.

Future of leadership? Well, the only thing we know about the future is that we do not know the future!

Only 12% of the Fortune 500 companies are still in business. This was the data of few years back. Interesting data and a point of concern too! There must have been huge learning on why 88% great companies disappeared from the list. Perceived opinion would rank 'collective failures' of leadership as key reason in those companies. Nevertheless, lessons from such data must already have forewarned the emerging leaders to review and renovate their leadership style.

India is already being seen as a reformist country with a tag of fastest growing economies. Forecast that India becoming a developed country by the time of centenary of Independence in 2047 no doubt a cause for exuberance but certainly not for celebration. While globally we are establishing our leadership in various fields, but locally we have still point of concern on various factors including tackling prevailing inequality in our socio - economic scenarios.

Government and other relevant forums are making their best efforts to address such key socio- economic issue. But we at corporates need to play more proactive the role in addressing such inequality. The corporate world needs mindset of reformative leadership. One important task towards that direction would be to make genuine efforts in transforming our own mind first before we make effort in transforming the business. Such leaders born or created should be nurtured and developed. Over a period of time, these leaders would be able to transform MSD (Minds, Souls and Deeds) of the people around them.

Research showed us that focus on health and education has paved the way for many poor societies to move up the radar of quicker growth. And I am sure that similar structured mission in the Corporate worlds would make huge difference.

How many organization's leadership 'think- tank' would burn that extra energy to think about social security focussing on their middle and bottom of the pyramid's people's kids? Creating small budget to begin with on such areas would bring mileage on higher returns beside the greatest satisfaction of contributing to building nation. Yes- there are organizations who are actively persuading such causes but they are too meagre a numbers.

While being on importance of education, let's recall Swami Vivekananda's view. It was around 130 years ago that Swamy ji after leaving the monastery as a Parivrajaka - the religious life of a wandering monk, moved around the entire country extensively on foot as part of his mission of Bharat Parikrama said that education is the panacea for all the evils that we encounter.

Once education becomes fundamental right of every children and emphasise begins with actioning it, the better we would contribute in creating future leaders in every mind, soul of the people.

How long we would hang upon the punchy punch lines of "people are our greatest assets" without 'walk-the-talk' in caring about them? How long corporates would focus on creating wealth creation scheme, profit sharing concept etc for the cream of the leadership team? Let's recognise that cream of the leadership talents could not have achieved their goals without the sweaty commitment of the people at the lower rung of the pyramid. Innovative financial budgets, even if it is low to begin with, linking it to productivity for such category is extremely important. These are only few examples that hovered around our mind and let the collective mind renovate more such simple but important tasks.

Well, we enjoy driving alongside the classy sky scrapers as such projects reflects our so called perceived phenomenal progress. But would not our soul be pained to see the co-existence of the slums next to such high ridges and the struggle of the slum dwellers in getting their "roti, kapra aur makan"?

Melody of the famous song of Bharat Ratna, Padma Bhusan and Padma Shri late Dr Bhupen Hazarika's "Ami ek jajabar ....." brings sonic experience in my ears and let me cite the relevant two lines of the lyric from that bong song –

"আমি দেখেছি অনেক গগনচুম্বী অট্টালিকার সারি

তার ছায়াতেই দেখেছি অনেক গৃহহীন নরনারী"

And the English translation would look like –

"I have seen many skyscrapers monuments and building's rows,

And I have seen countless homeless men – women in its shadows".

What a sharp contrast in our socio - economic scenario!

Added to these woes are growing hatred, vengeful minds, unhealthy competition, including growing number of companies being ridiculed in to controversy of unethical practises, integrity related issues. Minds of common people desires freedom from such repeated scam, systematic corruptions which are deeply rooted cancers in the body politic.

Are not those phenomenon of unethical leadership brings us to Shakespeare's Macbeth when the witches chant in Act 1 of scene 1 that "Fair is foul and foul is fair "?

Isn't it still being witnessed? Are not all these challenges appears to be growing threat to leadership ethos, values including culture, morale, brand images of the organizations?

Are these all due to erosion, deterioration of our ethical or moral judgements, righteousness? The challenges are enormous.

But amidst all those toughest hurdles, challenges, we have reasons to be confident in surging ahead. Global pandits also have been echoing similar confidence on our rapid progress.

Let's look at a relevant comments from Abraham Pinkusewitz **(****)**, the stalwart of the Diamond trading from Belgium when he shared – "Jews are good at business. But we cannot pursue it with the single-mindedness of the Indians. Indian managers have been exposed to unstructured situations early in life and these help them to learn special skills". Interesting indeed!

Interestingly, we have been mastering the art of 'copabiity' right from struggling in our early school admissions to getting in to the professional institutions. Parental pressure from early student's life has been soaking young minds to deal with toughest rat race of how to be competitive and that too amidst unstructured environment?

Well, maybe these are also perhaps bringing out devastatingly resilience aptitude. Toughest hurdles or setbacks right from student days won't deter our people. And all these also contributes to our becoming tomorrow's successful leaders.

I see lacs of aspirants but one aspiration – Kissing success! Highly encouraging. But we cannot solve our problems with the same thinking we used when we created them **(Albert Einstein ****).**

Tomorrow's leaders would certainly bring renaissance in leading organizations. But some of the traits and skills they need to be nurtured and get groomed would be:

- Develop attributes of righteousness - in other word, to be leader of character.
- Learn to control egos as at times it might dominate us affecting the outcome.
- Discovering one's own path through self-enlightenment as that would help to govern the outer world.
- No more boss? Yes - leaders won't be perceived any more as boss. But would be seen as mentors and facilitators.
- Future would be 'stake holder centred leadership'. It encompasses anchoring role of leaders in inspiring, bonding, helping discovering meaningfulness. Key would be on leaders proficiency in ideating how to strengthen people around them towards value added performance - **Marshall Goldsmith (****).**
- They must learn to develop their fundamentals of what they would emanate would have high impact on their surroundings.
- How quickly tomorrow's Leaders would internalize the importance of being trustworthy, down to earth, humble?
- Tomorrow's leadership would be - 'talking with the people', instead of today's pattern of 'talking about people'.

- 'Employee engagement'? Too ornamental. Too robotic. It would be the art and science of moving to 'engagement with people's mind, their emotions, their aspirations', listening and appreciating the causes of their success, failures, frustration and excitement.
- Capability to copability - Such skill will help them in navigating, dealing and taking control of complexities and uncertainties.
- Instead of conventional organization structure where the CEO is always at the top of pyramid and front line guys at the bottom of pyramid, tomorrow's market dynamics might provoke leaders to innovate organization structure where customers would remain at the top of pyramid. Their business strategy, their expectations, their feedback would drive the leadership team to steer organization from the bottom of pyramid.
- Tomorrow's leader might have to deal with dilemma on "Core Values – whether they are written on the rock or review and re - visit their Core Values "as the organizations would move to a newer world? **William Blake (****),** the English poet rightly said "The man who never alters his opinion is like standing water, and breeds reptiles of the mind".
- 14th **Dalai Lama (****)** opined: "Open your arms to change but don't let go of your Values". So, should we accept the fact that Values are eternal – they helps us to make our foundation more stronger? Debate would be going on.

A country with 140 crore of population might be having umpteen number of challenges, complexities, huge political differences of opinion so far leading the country is concerned. But on every occasion, when the national flag has to be unfurled, the country witnesses a huge vibration – a huge celebration – a huge solidarity, as if we are one soul – India. That's our DNA. It's strong enough to ensure that our ambition to lead, to flourish and be enriched in all aspects would never hit 'Cul-De-Sac', rather the world would enjoy and be able to grasp the alacrity of our emerging leadership.

And such vibration would enable corporate leadership too to be vision driven. Righteous corporate leadership would surely be contagious enough to radiate positive energy. Such vibes would be infectious enough to influence the energy that would flow down the line within each company. The task to constantly transform each mind is a journey. And it would enable every soul hums the tune of Great Atul Prasad Sen's patriotic song of:

"বল বল বল সবে

শত বীণা বেনু রবে,

ভারত আবার জগত সভায়

শ্রেষ্ঠ আসন লবে".

The essence of these lines in English would be –

"Let all my countrymen lend a voice to the melodies of hundreds of sitars and flutes –

Let them raise a voice echoing boldly that India will rise. That it shall acquire a title of grandest of them all"

And till then let's continue to get soaked with the spirit of – "What is that life's worth which cannot aspire us to inspire?"!

APPRECIATION

My gratitude to the partners during this journey who always had been supportive whenever I needed some help and they are:

Shreya Chaturvedi, Namrata Kumar ,Dikshita Dey, Prakash Panda, Jaydeep Chatterjee, Mithu Chakrabarty, Indrajit Gupta, Chandrima Banerjee, Surojit Kar, Nancy Gupta, Farhana, Debarshi, Dipanwita Sinha, Somash Roy, Debojo...

In the event inadvertently I have missed out some name, it would be unintentional.

www.ingramcontent.com/pod-product-compliance
Lightning Source LLC
LaVergne TN
LVHW091100150826
845673LV00002B/662

* 9 7 9 8 8 9 1 3 3 7 5 3 4 *